HARMONY

Books by Walter Piston

HARMONY

COUNTERPOINT

ORCHESTRATION

Walter Piston

PROFESSOR OF MUSIC, EMERITUS
HARVARD UNIVERSITY

HARMONY

Third Edition

 W · W · NORTON & COMPANY · INC · *New York*

Musical Illustrations Autographed by Mario Carmosino

SBN 393 09737 4

0

Contents

Preface to the Third Edition

IN THIS third edition the entire text has been reviewed. It has been reworded and expanded wherever it seemed that a clearer exposition of the author's meaning might be achieved. The addition of seventy-five new examples has improved the distribution of these as to media and composers represented. One hundred and seventy new exercises, mostly of a shorter, more introductory nature, are offered as preparation for the longer and more difficult exercises. The order of chapters has been altered slightly, for the purpose of giving the student earlier acquaintance with inversions of triads, and with nonharmonic tones.

A new final chapter presents a broader concept of tonality based on principles already learned, a wider view of the scope of a tonal center, needed for an approach to the study of harmony as used by composers of the twentieth century. Exercises are not given for this chapter, since it involves rather a question of harmonic analysis than one of new chords and their treatment. The points made will best be clarified through analysis of complete compositions.

The fundamental philosophy and principles upon which this study of harmony rests are unchanged and reaffirmed in the light of twenty years' use of the book in teaching. It is well to emphasize again that the primary concern is to provide an understanding of the common practice of composers, in matters of harmony, as observed in music of the eighteenth and nineteenth centuries. Such knowledge is essential not only for composers but for persons seriously interested in any aspect of music.

Introduction

THE first important step in the study of harmony is that of clarifying the purpose of such study. Much confusion exists today as to why we study musical theory and what we should expect to learn from it. In the present writer's teaching experience this confusion of outlook furnishes the commonest and most serious obstacle to progress in all branches of musical theory.

There are those who consider that studies in harmony, counterpoint, and fugue are the exclusive province of the intended composer. But if we reflect that theory must follow practice, rarely preceding it except by chance, we must realize that musical theory is not a set of directions for composing music. It is rather the collected and systematized deductions gathered by observing the practice of composers over a long time, and it attempts to set forth what is or has been their common practice. It tells not how music will be written in the future, but how music has been written in the past.

The results of such a definition of the true nature of musical theory are many and important. First of all, it is clear that this knowledge is indispensable to musicians in all fields of the art, whether they be composers, performers, conductors, critics, teachers, or musicologists. Indeed, a secure grounding in theory is even more a necessity to the musical scholar than to the composer, since it forms the basis for any intelligent appraisal of individual styles of the past or present.

On the other hand, the person gifted for creative musical compositon is taking a serious risk in assuming that his genius is great enough to get along without a deep knowledge of the common practice of composers. Mastery of the technical or theoretical aspects of music should be carried out by him as a life's work, running parallel to his creative activity but quite separate from it. In the one he is following common practice, while in the other he is responsible solely to the dictates of his own personal tastes and urge for expression.

In the specific field of harmony we must first seek the answer to two questions—what are the harmonic materials commonly used by composers, and how have these materials been used? We cannot afford in the first stages of our study to become interested in the individual composer at the expense of concentration on establishing the norm of common practice. With such a norm firmly in mind, the way will be clear to the investigation of the individual harmonic practices of composers of all periods, and especially to the scientific examination of the divergent practices noticeable in the twentieth century.

Historically, the period in which this common practice may be detected includes roughly the eighteenth and nineteenth centuries. During that time there is surprisingly little change in the harmonic materials used and in the manner of their use. The experimental period of the early twentieth century will appear far less revolutionary when the lines of development from the practice of older composers become clearer by familiarity with the music. As yet, however, one cannot define a twentieth-century common practice.

Hence the aim of this book is to present as concisely as possible the harmonic common practice of composers of the eighteenth and nineteenth centuries. Rules are announced as observations reported, without attempt at their justification on aesthetic grounds or as laws of nature. The written exercises should be performed as exemplifications of the common practice of composers and not as efforts in creative composition. The author believes that through these principles a prompt and logical grasp of the subject will be achieved.

HARMONY

One | SCALES AND INTERVALS

THE unit of harmony is the interval. This name refers to the sonority resulting from the simultaneous sounding of two tones, although it is more accurately used to describe the "distance" between the two tones, measured by their difference in pitch. If the two tones are not heard at the same time, but are consecutive tones of one melodic line, the interval is called a melodic interval, as distinguished from the harmonic interval, in which the two tones are sounded together.

EX. 1

harmonic interval   melodic interval

The tones which form the interval are drawn from the scale. Three scales are used as the basis of the music with which we are here concerned—the major scale, the minor scale (with its harmonic and melodic forms), and the chromatic scale.

EX. 2

major scale

I   II   III   IV   V   VI   VII   I   VII   VI   V   IV   III   II   I

harmonic minor scale

I   II   III   IV   V   VI   VII   I   VII   VI   V   IV   III   II   I

melodic minor scale

I   II   III   IV   V   VI   VII   I   VII   VI   V   IV   III   II   I

chromatic scale

I   II   III IV   V   VI   VII I VII   VI   V   IV III   II   I

It is customary to refer to the scale degrees by Roman numerals as in the example, as well as by the following names:

I. Tonic (the key-note)

II. Supertonic (the next step above the tonic)

III. Mediant (halfway from tonic to dominant)

IV. Subdominant (as far below the tonic as the dominant is above it)

V. Dominant (actually a dominant element in the key)

VI. Submediant (halfway down from tonic to subdominant)

VII. Leading-tone (with melodic tendency toward the tonic)

The scales are distinguished by the distribution of half-tone and whole-tone steps, recognition of which is assumed on the part of readers of this book. The chromatic scale, having its origin in the chromatic alteration of tones, is most conveniently considered as a variant of one of the other scales, as shown by the Roman numerals. The proper notation of this scale (for instance, whether one should write A-sharp or B-flat) is determined by melodic and harmonic circumstances to be considered later.

The melodic minor scale may likewise be looked upon as variant of the harmonic form. In ascending, the characteristic sixth degree is changed, so that the step greater than a whole-tone between VI and VII is eliminated, while preserving the half-tone progression from leading-tone to tonic. In descending, the seventh degree no longer acts as leading-tone, so it is lowered to reduce the step down to the minor sixth degree.

It is important to notice that the major and minor (harmonic) scales differ only in their III and VI.

CLASSIFICATION OF INTERVALS

The general name of an interval is found by counting the lines and spaces included by the two notes.

EX. 3

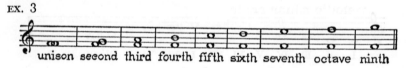

unison second third fourth fifth sixth seventh octave ninth

The specific name of an interval (the kind of 3rd, 7th, etc.) may be found by various methods, a simple one being to compare the interval to a major scale constructed upon the lower of the two notes as a tonic. If the upper note coincides with a note of the scale, the interval is "major," except in the case of octaves, fifths, fourths, and unisons, for which the term "perfect" is used.

EX. 4

| | perf. | maj. | maj. | perf. | perf. | maj. | maj. | perf. |
Eb major scale | unison | 2nd | 3rd | 4th | 5th | 6th | 7th | 8ve.

If the upper note does not coincide with a note of the scale, the following considerations are to be applied.

a. A major interval made a half-tone smaller, by chromatically lowering its upper note or raising its lower note, becomes "minor." Conversely, a minor interval made chromatically a half-tone larger becomes "major."

b. A major interval, or a perfect interval, made chromatically a half-tone larger becomes "augmented."

c. A minor interval, or a perfect interval, made chromatically a half-tone smaller becomes "diminished."

EX. 5

aug. 6th   min. 3rd   aug. 2nd   aug. 4th   min. 7th

In the above example, consider the interval of a sixth, E-flat to C-sharp. If the C had been natural it would have fallen in the scale of E-flat major and the interval would have been a major sixth. The sharp, by raising the top note, has the effect of making a major interval a half-tone larger. Therefore, statement *b* in the paragraph above is applied, and the interval is called an "augmented sixth."

When the lower note is preceded by a sharp or flat, the interval may be analyzed first without the sharp or flat, and the result compared with the original interval by reference to the above rules. For example, suppose the interval to be from D-sharp up to C. The scale of D-sharp major, with nine sharps, is not convenient as a measuring device. Taking the scale of D major, we find that C is a half-tone short of the seventh degree. The interval D to C is therefore a minor seventh. The restoration of the sharp to the D makes the interval a half-tone smaller, by raising the lower note; hence it is a diminished seventh.

The student is urged to perfect himself, by exercises in dictation or other processes of ear-training, in the ability to recognize the intervals by ear when they are played or sung, and to hear mentally intervals written or printed.

COMPOUND INTERVALS

An interval greater than the octave may be reckoned by subtracting the octave. Such intervals are called compound intervals. Some of these, however, for example the ninth, are characteristic features of certain harmonic forms and are usually called by the larger number.

EX. 6
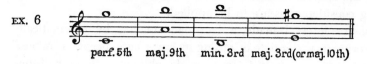

perf. 5th   maj. 9th   min. 3rd   maj. 3rd(or maj. 10th)

CONSONANT AND DISSONANT INTERVALS

A consonant interval is one which sounds stable and complete, whereas the characteristic of the dissonant interval is its restlessness and its need for resolution into a consonant interval. These qualities are admittedly open to subjective, personal, and evolutionary interpretation but it is clear that in the common practice of composers the following classification holds true.

Consonant—the perfect intervals and the major and minor thirds and sixths.

Dissonant—the augmented and diminished intervals and the major and minor seconds, sevenths, and ninths.

(Exception—the perfect fourth is dissonant when there is no tone below its lower tone. It is consonant when there is a third or perfect fifth below it.)

EX. 7

dissonant 4th   consonant 4th

The major and minor thirds and sixths are frequently set apart from the perfect intervals and termed "imperfect consonances." This distinction has little significance for the harmonic style of the eighteenth and nineteenth centuries. Only the sixth, when in certain tonal rela-

tionships with the bass, seems to lack the stability of the perfect consonances and to need resolution to the fifth.

EX. 8

Music without dissonant intervals is often lifeless and negative,
since it is the dissonant element which furnishes much of the sense
of movement and rhythmic energy. The history of musical style has
been largely occupied with the important subject of dissonance and
its treatment by composers. It cannot be too strongly emphasized that
the essential quality of dissonance is its sense of movement and not,
as sometimes erroneously assumed, its degree of unpleasantness to the
ear.

INVERSION OF INTERVALS

The term "inversion" is somewhat loosely applied in music to a
variety of procedures. True inversion, of course, means that the original
interval and its inversion are of equal size but extending in opposite
directions from a common point. The systematic application of this is
what is called "mirror-writing" and is not often found in the music of
the harmonic common-practice period.

EX. 9

maj. 6th inversion melodic group inversion

Ordinary contrapuntal inversion, which is common, is a modifica-
tion of the mirror type. Here the same scale is kept for both forms,
so that while each interval and its inversion have the same general
name, the specific names may be different on account of the place
in the scale occupied by each.

EX. 10

melodic group in E♭ major inversion

Harmonic inversion is quite a different matter. In this procedure
the names of the notes remain the same, but the lower of the two

becomes the upper, or vice versa, with the consequence that there is usually a change in both the general and specific names of the interval.

EX. 11

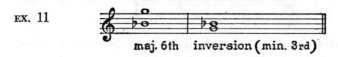

maj. 6th   inversion (min. 3rd)

ENHARMONIC INTERVALS

In our tempered scale system it often happens that two or more intervals sound alike when played on the pianoforte, even though they are widely different in their meaning. A good example is the augmented second, which cannot be distinguished from the minor third without further evidence than the sound of the two tones. One interval is called the enharmonic equivalent of the other.

EX. 12

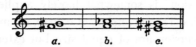

a.   *b.*   *c.*

When these intervals are heard in their harmonic context, however, their difference becomes clearly audible.

EX. 13

a.   *b.*   *c.*

EXERCISES

The exercises offered in this book are intended as specimens or suggestions for further exercises to be invented by the teacher or by the student himself. They do not pretend to supply adequate practice or training. It goes without saying that the material in each chapter must be thoroughly assimilated before proceeding to the next. The exercises must be multiplied until that end is achieved.

1. Name the following intervals:

2. With F-sharp as the lower tone, construct these intervals: min. 3rd; aug. 6th; dim. 5th; perf. 4th; aug. 2nd; maj. 7th; min. 9th; aug. 5th.

3. With D-flat as the upper tone, construct these intervals: dim. 5th; maj. 9th; dim. 7th; min. 2nd; aug. 4th; perf. 5th; min. 6th; dim. 3rd.

4. Write enharmonic equivalents of the intervals in Ex. 3.

5. From what scales may the following fragments have been taken?

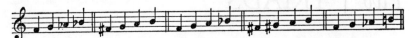

6. Construct a major scale in which C-sharp is the sixth degree.

7. Construct a descending melodic minor scale with D as the tonic.

8. Name the interval from supertonic up to submediant in the harmonic minor scale.

9. Write and name the dissonant intervals which may be formed between the tonic and other tones of the scale of E major.

10. Write and name the consonant intervals which may be formed between the third degree and other tones of the harmonic minor scale of B-flat.

Supplementary exercises for this chapter and for the succeeding chapters will be found at the conclusion of the text, commencing on page 338.

$\mathcal{T}wo$ | TRIADS

THE combination of two or more harmonic intervals makes a chord. Chords are ordinarily built by superposing intervals of a third. While it would be instructive to experiment with other ways of combining intervals, and to see how these experiments have been applied in twentieth century music, we must confine our studies here to the chords used in the common practice of composers.

The simplest chord is the triad, a chord of three tones obtained by the superposition of two thirds. The triad may be said to be the basis of our whole harmonic system, a place it still holds despite numerous radical contemporary developments.

The names "root," "third," and "fifth" are given to the three factors of the triad. The root is also called the "fundamental." These terms are retained to identify the factors of the triad in whatever order they may be arranged.

EX. 14
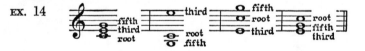

INVERSIONS

A triad with its root as its lowest tone is said to be in root position.

A triad with its third as its lowest tone is said to be in the first inversion.

10

A triad with its fifth as its lowest tone is said to be in the second inversion.

EX. 15

root position first inversion second inversion

Taking the two scales, major and harmonic minor, of the tonic C, and using only the notes of these scales, superposition of thirds gives the following triads:

EX. 16

KINDS OF TRIADS

The triads formed on a given scale differ not only in pitch but also, depending on the intervals in their make-up, in the quality of their sound. There are four kinds of triads, classified according to the nature of the intervals formed between the root and the other two tones.

A major triad is composed of major third and perfect fifth.

A minor triad is composed of minor third and perfect fifth.

An augmented triad is composed of major third and augmented fifth.

A diminished triad is composed of minor third and diminished fifth.

The student should learn by practice to distinguish by ear the four types of triads.

EX. 17

maj. min. aug. dim.

The major and minor triads are consonant chords because they contain only consonant intervals. The diminished and augmented triads, on the other hand, are dissonant because of the presence of the dissonant intervals, diminished fifth and augmented fifth.

Roman numerals identify not only the scale degree but also the chord constructed upon that scale degree as a root, whether the chord is in root position or in an inversion.

EX. 18

C: V   V   II   II   IV   IV

Considering the entire group of triads the following observations may be made:

The major triads are: I, IV, V in the major mode;
V, VI in the minor mode.

The minor triads are: II, III, VI in the major mode;
I, IV in the minor mode.

The diminished triads are: VII in the major mode;
VII, II in the minor mode.

There is but one augmented triad—III in the minor mode.

Or, from the point of view of the scale degrees:

I is a major triad in the major mode, minor in the minor mode.

II is a minor triad in the major mode, diminished in the minor mode.

III is a minor triad in the major mode, augmented in the minor mode.

IV is a major triad in the major mode, minor in the minor mode.

V is a major triad in both modes.

VI is a minor triad in the major mode, major in the minor mode.

VII is a diminished triad in both modes.

Most music of the eighteenth and nineteenth centuries is conceived on a harmonic basis of four-part writing. This means vertically four factors in each chord, and horizontally four different melodic voices. The three-part writing often observed in the classics frequently suggests four voices, whereas larger numbers of apparent parts, as for instance in an orchestral score, are usually the result of reduplication of one or more voices in a basically four-part texture.

The study of harmony is concerned with the principles underlying the construction of this common basis of four-part writing. The exercises are ordinarily worked out in four voices. The term "voices" does not necessarily mean that the parts are to be sung. It does suggest, however, that the separate parts proceed with a certain ideal vocal quality which is possessed by all good melodic music, whether intended for human voices or for instruments.

In order to define these four parts, or voices, we shall follow the usual custom of naming them for the four classes of singing voices— soprano, alto, tenor, and bass—somewhat arbitrarily restricting their ranges to an approximation of the ranges of human voices.

EX. 19

soprano   alto   tenor   bass

There is no harm in exceeding these limits occasionally, as long as the balance or "center of gravity" of each voice remains well within its normal range, and extreme notes are sparingly employed.

DOUBLING

Since the triad contains but three tones, it is evident that another is needed for four-part harmony. With triads in root position, the fourth tone is customarily a duplication of the root an octave or two higher, or even at the unison. This is called doubling.

SPACING

One rarely hears music that is purely harmonic, in which the vertical effect is free from modifications due to horizontal, or melodic, influences. These considerations, the principles of voice leading, always take precedence over considerations of the chord as such, since chords themselves have their origin in the coincidence of melodic movement. At the same time, the harmonic sense demands an arrangement of the vertical sonority which will give clarity and balance, and even on occasion such subjective qualities as beauty, brilliance, or somberness.

The commonest arrangement of a chord places the wide intervals at the bottom, with the smallest intervals at the top. This bears a resemblance, as has often been pointed out, to the distribution of overtones in the harmonic series, but it must be admitted that the parallel between the usage of composers and the "chord of nature" stops there. Compare, for instance, a triad in first inversion with the series of overtones generated by its lowest tone.

EX. 20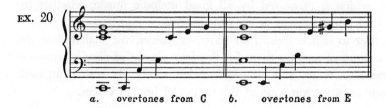

a.   overtones from C   b.   overtones from E

Intervals wider than the octave are usually avoided between soprano and alto, and between alto and tenor, but are considered quite satisfactory between tenor and bass.

EX. 21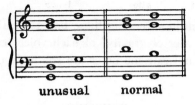

unusual   normal

CLOSE AND OPEN POSITION

When the three upper voices are as close together as possible, the spacing is described as close position. Otherwise the chord is in open position, provided all four normal factors are present. It will be noticed that in close position the three upper voices are all within the range of a single octave, whereas in open position there is a distance of more than an octave between soprano and tenor. In arranging a root position triad in close position, having a given soprano note, the alto will take the next immediately available chord note below the soprano. If open position is desired, the alto will not take this first available note, but will take the next below. The tenor will fall into place with the only note left, as the bass will of course take the root, in whatever octave is convenient.

EX. 22

close   open

Close and open position are of equally common use. The choice of one or the other is subject to various conditions, among which melodic progress of the parts is perhaps the most important. Another is the question of ranges. If the soprano voice is in a high register, for example, close position may result in placing the other voices too high. The ideal of balance in a single chord would be to have all voices in corresponding registers all high, all medium, or all low, but this is seldom possible of achievement because of melodic direction and other influential considerations.

One should listen carefully to the relative effect of various spacings of the same chord and notice the kind of spacing used in music heard. The intervals between the voices are an important factor in the texture and actual sound of the music. In the common-practice period of harmonic usage this has been largely a matter of effective distribution of given chord tones, but, with the twentieth century, composers have become much more preoccupied with intervals and their combination into individual sonorities.

EXERCISES

1. The teacher will play a scale, major or minor, and afterwards a triad derived from that scale. The student will tell the kind of triad and the scale degree which is its root.

One cannot overestimate the value of this type of ear-training exercise. Facility can be gained only through regular practice, with the aid of another person to do the playing. The most satisfactory and feasible method is to get together a small group of interested students and let each take a turn at the piano.

2. Identify the following triads as to kind (major, minor, diminished, or augmented), and indicate by Roman numerals and key their possible derivations as to scale and degree. (For example, the first triad given is major, IV of B major, or I of E major, etc.)

a.   b.   c.   d.   e.   f.   g.   h.   i.   j.

3. Write three different spacings in four parts of each of the following triads:

    a.   *b.*   *c.*   *d.*   *e.*

4. Write in four parts, in both close and open position, the following triads:

        a. IV in B-flat minor
        b. V in C-sharp major
        c. VI in E major
        d. III in D minor
        e. II in F minor
        f. IV in A major
        g. I in E-flat minor
        h. VI in E minor
        i. VII in G major
        j. II in A-flat major

5. By the use of accidentals only (sharps, flats, or naturals), write each of the following triads in three additional ways, altering them so as to illustrate in each case the four types, major, minor, augmented, and diminished:

    a.   *b.*   *c.*   *d.*   *e.*

Three | HARMONIC PROGRESSION

W HEN chords are to be heard in succession there are two main questions to be considered. The first is the choice of the chord to follow a given chord, and the second is the procedure to be followed in connecting the two chords. These are two aspects of what is known as harmonic progression.

Although these two questions are in a sense inseparable, the matter of succession can be regarded as independent of the forms of the chords themselves. As more of these forms are studied it will be more and more apparent that the individual sonority of the two chords is of less importance than the relation of the two roots to each other and to the scale from which they are drawn. Chords are identified primarily by their situation in the tonality or, in other words, by the scale degree serving as root. Hence chord succession can be reduced to root succession (or root progression), which in turn can be translated into Roman numerals representing a succession of scale degrees. The variety of chords built upon these roots cannot alter this relationship, and no change in the make-up of the chords can remedy an inappropriate root progression.

The following generalizations are based on observation of usage, with no attempt to justify usage by suggesting reasons of an acoustical nature (although such physical hypotheses surely do exist). They are not proposed as a set of strict rules to be rigidly adhered to.

17

TABLE OF USUAL ROOT PROGRESSIONS

I is followed by IV or V, sometimes VI, less often II or III.
II is followed by V, sometimes VI, less often I, III, or IV.
III is followed by VI, sometimes IV, less often II or V.
IV is followed by V, sometimes I or II, less often III or VI.
V is followed by I, sometimes VI or IV, less often III or II.
VI is followed by II or V, sometimes III or IV, less often I.
VII is followed by III, sometimes I.

It is important to form an appreciation of the qualities of these progressions, qualities which do not readily lend themselves to description by words. The dominant-to-tonic progression is generally considered the most satisfying. One can easily sense the repose of this progression by playing the bass alone.

EX. 23

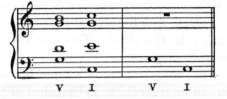

V   I   V   I

Other progressions with root moving down a fifth (or up a fourth) seem to have an analogous effect, although in less marked degree.

EX. 24

VI   II   II   V   III   VI   I   IV

Root movement down a fourth (or up a fifth) gives the reverse of those above. Comparison shows the effect to be distinctly different.

EX. 25

I   V   II   VI   V   II   VI   III   IV   I

When the root proceeds by step, the second chord will consist of a completely new set of notes, and hence will have the effect of introducing a new harmonic color.

EX. 26

IV V   III IV   VI V   III II

A contrast to this is the soft effect when the root moves up a third. In this case the root of the second chord has just been heard as the third of the first chord. On the other hand, when the root descends a third, the root of the second chord comes as a new note.

EX. 27

I III   IV VI   IV II   III I

THE LEADING-TONE TRIAD

The triad on the seventh degree is rarely found in root position and can safely be omitted from the discussion of root progression. It contains a dissonant interval, the diminished fifth, the lower tone of which is the leading-tone itself, with its strong tendency toward the tonic. In its action and effect this triad is really an incomplete dominant seventh chord and is so treated. As a rule, doubling of the leading-tone is avoided.

Occasionally one finds the leading-tone triad progressing to III, usually in a sequential pattern where the chord, as well as the doubled leading-tone, may be used in order to preserve the symmetry of the voices.

EX. 28

II   V   I   IV   VII   III

THE SECOND DEGREE IN MINOR

The diminished triad formed on the second degree of the minor scale has the same dissonant interval as the leading-tone triad, the diminished fifth. However, the lower of the two tones is not in itself a tendency tone, and it has been the practice of composers to use this chord rather freely in root position.

EX. 29

C minor: II   V

THE AUGMENTED TRIAD

Another triad with a dissonant interval is that on the third degree of the harmonic minor scale. In this case there is an augmented fifth between the root and the leading-tone. It is usual to double the third of this triad, that being the fifth degree, dominant, of the scale.

EX. 30

A minor: III   VI

Each progression possesses certain rhythmic values, to be discussed in a later chapter.

VOICE LEADING

Having decided what the root succession is to be, the next question is how the two chords are connected, that is, how the voices move horizontally.

The following observations describe the procedure followed to connect two triads in root position. Notice that what is sought particularly is smoothness of melodic movement from chord to chord. For this

reason augmented intervals are as a rule avoided in melodic progression as being somewhat awkward.

1. If the two triads have one or more notes in common, these are usually repeated in the same voice, the remaining voice or voices moving to the nearest available position.

EX. 31

C: I   V

In the example, G is a common tone of both triads, so it is repeated in the same voice, the alto. The other two voices move to the nearest position available—C down to B, E to D. (The notes of the second chord are G, B, D, G. The two G's have been used, one by the bass since that is the root, and the other by the repeated alto. Therefore B and D are the only available tones.) If C had gone to D, E would have been forced to take B, the only note left, and this would not have been to the nearest position.

Exception: In the progression II–V, it is customary not to repeat the common tone but to move the three upper voices down to the next available position.

EX. 32

II   V   II   V   II   V

In the minor mode, repeating the common tone in II–V would cause one of the voices to move by an augmented second.

EX. 33

II   V   II   V
avoided   accepted

2. If the two triads have no tones in common, the upper three voices proceed in the opposite direction to the bass, always to the nearest available position.

EX. 34

IV   V   II   III   III   IV

Exception: In the progression V–VI, the leading-tone moves up one degree to the tonic, while the other two voices descend to the nearest position in the chord, doubling the third, instead of the root, in the triad on VI.

EX. 35

V   VI   V   VI   minor: V   VI

L.T.=leading tone

If the directions given above are followed, the connection between the chords will be correct according to the practice of voice leading in harmonic progression. The purpose of this procedure is to insure the smoothest possible connection of two chords, so that one seems to flow into the next. Continued application of the process will, however, result in rather dull music.

EX. 36

F: I VI IV V   III VI IV II   V VI IV V   I

One does not expect fine four-part contrapuntal writing in the first studies of root position triads. Moreover, the emphasis in harmonic study will, of necessity, be directed to the chords. But the cultivation and exercise of musical taste and judgment are implicit in the effort to emulate the practice of composers. It is never too early to insist on the constant seeking for what is truly musical. Even in the exercises dealing with such elementary material as root position triads, there will always exist the possibility of an arrangement that is a little more interesting and musical than another.

In other words, the set of rules is broken whenever greater musical interest can be achieved by breaking them, and this will be noticeable first of all in the soprano line. The soprano, being the top line, is instinctively heard as a melody and so must receive more care in its construction than the inside voices.

When the root is repeated it is advisable to change the position of the other voices, for variety.

EX. 37

A change from open to close position, or vice versa, is often a good way to obtain a new soprano note.

EX. 38

The occasional use of a triad without fifth, usually composed of three roots and one third, may help to free the soprano line. It is not advisable to omit the third, as that leaves the empty sound of the open fifth.

EX. 39

Doubling of the third or fifth instead of the root is another means of making more notes available for the soprano part.

EX. 40

    IV   I   V   VI

Rhythmic division of some notes of the soprano into smaller time values is a frequent resource in the making of a melody, as is likewise the tying over of possible repeated notes to make notes of larger time values. The student is advised to use this device sparingly at first, in order to gain experience in the vertical arrangement of the chords before adding rhythmic complications.

EX. 41

    I VI   IV V   I   V

As by various means the voices are given more freedom of movement, attention must be given to the ways in which they may move, both as regards their individual melodic lines and their relative melodic progression. The terms "conjunct" and "disjunct" motion are used to describe the movement of a single line by step and by skip respectively.

EX. 42

        conjunct   disjunct

A good melodic line contains mostly conjunct motion, with the disjunct motion used judiciously for variety. Too many skips make for angularity rather than for the desired flowing quality. It will be noticed that basses are likely to contain more skips than the other parts, while the alto and tenor as a rule have few, if any, large disjunct intervals. In using only triads in root position the bass will necessarily be more disjunct than is ordinarily desirable.

RELATIVE MOTION

Two voices may move relatively in three ways: in contrary motion; in oblique motion; or in similar motion.

Contrary motion, the voices moving in opposite directions:

EX. 43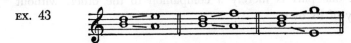

Oblique motion, one voice level while the other moves:

EX. 44

Similar motion, both voices moving in the same direction:

EX. 45

In similar motion, if the two voices keep the same distance apart they are said to be in parallel motion. Two voices moving in parallel motion are melodically less independent than otherwise, and may be looked upon as a single voice with reduplication. Parallel intervals of the unison, octave, and perfect fifth have been systematically avoided by the composers of the eighteenth and nineteenth centuries, whenever it has been their intention to write a basic four-part texture.

EX. 46

   unisons   octaves   perfect fifths

Parallel thirds and sixths are common. Parallel fourths are used if supported by parallel thirds below.

EX. 47

              avoided   accepted

Parallel dissonant intervals occur in certain circumstances arising from the use of contrapuntal nonharmonic tones and irregular resolutions of dissonant chords.

The relative motion of the voices is planned to preserve their independence as separate parts. The maximum of independence is furnished by contrary motion, but it is obviously not possible for four parts to move in four different directions. Oblique motion is useful to contrast a moving voice with one that is standing still. In similar motion care must be taken that the movement is not so consistently similar that one part is merely a companion to the other, without individuality of its own.

THE DIRECT OCTAVE AND FIFTH

Composers seem to have been careful about any approach by similar motion to the intervals of octave and perfect fifth. While such matters are more in the domain of the study of counterpoint, the prominence of these intervals when between the outside voices, bass and soprano, necessitates recognition of the practice.

An octave or a perfect fifth is not usually approached by similar motion, with skips in both voices. This combination is often referred to as hidden octaves, or hidden fifths, but the terms "direct octave" and "direct fifth" will be employed here.

EX. 48

In the case of the direct octave, it is usually avoided in upward movement even when one part moves by step, except when the upper voice moves by a minor second, acting as a leading-tone.

EX. 49

avoided   avoided   avoided   accepted

THE TRITONE

The interval of the augmented fourth is called the tritone, *i.e.*, three whole-tones. It has a peculiar kind of sound and it was looked upon with disfavor in the contrapuntal era, when it was referred to as *diabolus in musica.* The roughness of its effect was softened or avoided with consistent skill. In the period of common harmonic practice there seems to be but one form of the tritone that was nearly always shunned by composers. This is in the progression V–IV in root position. The leading-tone in V and the bass of IV are in relation of tritone, and here the term "cross-relation," or "false relation," is used to express the relationship between two successive tones which do not occur melodically in the same voice. The false relation of the tritone is easily heard in V–IV when the leading-tone is in the soprano voice, proceeding to the tonic, but is constantly used when the leading-tone is in either alto or tenor.

EX. 50

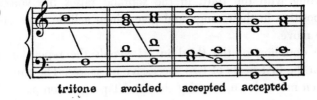

tritone   avoided   accepted   accepted

OVERLAPPING VOICES

When two voices move upwards in similar motion, the lower voice is not usually allowed to move to a position higher than that just left by the upper voice. This avoids ambiguity to the ear, which might follow an apparent melodic progression between the two voices. The corresponding rule holds for descending movement.

EX. 51

overlapping   not overlapping

In writing exercises in four parts, using two staves, the tenor should be written on the lower staff with the bass, so that the four voices can be readily seen as lines. It is also an aid to clarity to adopt the practice of pointing the stems of the soprano and tenor parts up, and those of alto and bass down.

At least two versions should be made of the exercises which call for a considerable number of chords. The first version should follow closely the steps outlined under the heading of voice leading, even though the result is as poor melodically as in Ex. 36. This will help to familiarize the student with the principles of connection of triads and will then serve as a basis for the departures necessary to obtain a better soprano line.

These departures need not be numerous or radical.

EX. 52

a. Starting with the third in the soprano raises the voices to a middle position in their range and gives them a little more space in which to move.

b. The doubling of the third in III avoids the repetition of the note A on the first beats of two successive measures. The three upper voices then move down, treating the III–VI progression as analogous to II–V.

c. The chord VI has its third doubled, as always in the progression V–VI. This gives a choice of repeating the common tone F in either tenor or soprano, as well as offering an opportunity of changing from close to open position.

The following is a third version of the same series of triads. The departures from the basic procedure should be analyzed by the student.

EX. 53

EXERCISES

1. Write, in four parts, three different arrangements of each of the following harmonic progressions, in root position:

    a. V–VI in E minor
    b. IV–V in D major
    c. I–VI in F major
    d. VI–V in C major
    e. V–I in A minor
    f. II–V in E-flat minor
    g. VI–IV in B-flat major
    h. II–V in F-sharp major
    i. III–VI in C-sharp minor
    j. V–VI in D-flat major

2. Write two versions of each of the following series of triads in root position. The first version should comply strictly with the stated rules for connecting triads, while the second should contain departures from the first in order to obtain a good melodic soprano part.

    a. C major: IV, V, I, I, V, VI, IV, II, V, V, I
    b. C minor: I, VI, IV, II, V, VI, IV, V, I, V, I
    c. A major: I, V, III, VI, IV, V, I, V, IV, IV, V, I
    d. B minor: V, I, IV, II, III, VI, IV, V, VI, IV, I

3. Add soprano, alto, and tenor parts to the following basses, using triads in root position. Make two versions of each bass as in the preceding exercise.

Four | TONALITY AND MODALITY

TONALITY is the organized relationship of tones in music. This relationship, as far as the common practice of composers in the eighteenth and nineteenth centuries is concerned, implies a central tone with all other tones supporting it or tending toward it, in one way or another. Earlier organizing principles, based on the modes, antedate the period we are studying.

Modality refers to the choice of the tones between which this relationship exists. Tonality is synonymous with key, modality with scale. In addition to the major, minor, and chromatic scales, an extremely large number of modes can be constructed in any given tonality. As illustration a few are given here on the key-note C.

EX. 54

These modes may be transposed into all tonalities, simply by changing the pitch of the tonic note and preserving the interval relationships.

EX. 55

Many modes taken from folk songs and even oriental scales have been used occasionally by composers. Artificial scales have been invented, containing a distribution of intervals not known before. But all of these must await investigation until the first task in the study of harmony is accomplished, namely the clear and firm establishment of the norm of common practice by reference to which these extraordinary resources are to be appreciated. We limit ourselves, therefore, to the three modes or scales described in Chapter One —major, minor, and chromatic, the last considered as a variant of the other two.

The acknowledged authority of these two modes over a period of some three hundred years has given rise to the expression "major-minor system" often applied to our music. We are so imbued with this tradition that we tend to interpret music based on other modes as being in either major or minor, usually with somewhat unsatisfactory results. How often it is that the ear accepts the impression of C major at the opening of the second movement of Brahms' Fourth Symphony, only to find soon afterward that E is the tonal center.

EX. 56. Brahms—*Fourth Symphony*

Instances like the above, of use of modes other than major and minor, are fairly numerous during the harmonic period but are by no means frequent enough to be called common practice. Such resources, drawn from earlier periods, were not even partially exploited again until the twentieth century. Further than the brief descriptive reference given here, modes other than major and minor will not be treated in this book.

TONAL FUNCTIONS OF THE SCALE DEGREES

Tonality, then, is not merely a matter of using just the tones of a particular scale. It is more a process of setting forth the organized relationship of these tones to one among them which is to be the tonal center. Each scale degree has its part in the scheme of tonality, its tonal function.

It is not the place here to attempt to outline the acoustic and psychological origins of these tonal functions. Let it suffice to report their existence as evidenced in the usage of composers.

Dominant and subdominant seem to give an impression of balanced support of the tonic, like two equidistant weights on either side of a fulcrum.

EX. 57

$$I \quad V \quad I \quad IV \quad I$$

The above could represent the scheme of harmonic progress of many a short piece of music, the first objective being the dominant, followed by return to the tonic, and then introduction of the subdominant to make the last tonic more satisfying and final. Other degrees are used to amplify and decorate this design.

Tonic, dominant, and subdominant are called the *tonal degrees,* since they are the mainstay of the tonality. In a given tonality these degrees remain the same for both modes.

EX. 58

C major I   IV   V   C minor I   IV   V

Mediant and submediant are called the *modal degrees.* They have very little effect on the tonality but suggest the mode, since they are different in major and minor.

EX. 59

The supertonic is most often treated as dominant of the dominant.

EX. 60

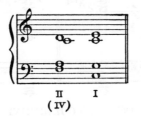

Harmonically, however, the supertonic often tends to become absorbed into the subdominant chord, especially in certain positions, and is sometimes spoken of as a substitute for the subdominant.

EX. 61

The supertonic should, therefore, be included in the list of tonal degrees, since it partakes of both dominant and subdominant characteristics, but should be distinguished from I, IV, and V, as having much less tonal strength.

The seventh degree, leading-tone, for all its importance as an indicator of the tonic through its melodic tendency, has not been treated as a basic structural factor in tonality. It remains a significant melodic tone, common to both modes. It is seldom regarded as a generator of harmony, but is usually absorbed into the dominant chord. The progression, leading-tone to tonic, may be described as melodically VII–I and harmonically V–I.

In terms of harmonic roots, overemphasis on the modal degrees tends to give the effect of a mode, and tonality, other than that intended. The modal degrees, by their insistence, are accepted by the ear as tonal degrees of another scale.

EX. 62

C: I   III   VI   II   III   IV   II   VI   III   V   I
  (V   I   IV   V   VI   IV   I   V)
A:Aeolian

It follows that the tonal structure of music consists mainly of harmonies with tonal degrees as roots (I, IV, V, and II), with the modal degree chords (III and VI) used for variety. It is interesting to note how in a single tonic chord one third degree is sufficient to "color" any number of doublings of the two tonal degrees and to explain the mode.

EX. 63

DOMINANT HARMONY

The strongest tonal factor in music is the dominant effect. Standing alone, it determines the key much more decisively than the tonic chord itself. This fact is perhaps not apparent with simple triads but should be borne in mind throughout the study of harmony. The addition of dissonances and chromatic alterations creates tendency tones which serve to augment the feeling of tonality inherent in the combination of leading-tone and dominant root. Establishment of a key by means of one of the many forms of dominant harmony is an everyday occurrence.

EX. 64 Beethoven—*Symphony no. 3*

Allegro molto

E♭: V of III   III   V

EX. 65 Chopin—*Prelude, op. 28, no. 16*

EX. 66 Mozart—*Sonata, K. 280*

EX. 67. Franck—*Sonata for Violin and Piano*

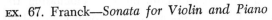

It has been thought desirable and proper to include symbols of harmonic analysis with the examples, even though some of these symbols may not be immediately understood by the reader. All such indications will be clarified in subsequent chapters.

TONAL STRENGTH OF CHORDS

A single chord heard by itself is capable of a number of interpretations as to its tonality.

EX. 68

F: I   E: I
Bᵇ: V   G: VI
C: IV   C: III
A: VI   B: IV

This ambiguity, which will later prove advantageous to the process of modulation, is greatly lessened when two chords are heard in a harmonic progression. The progressions have in themselves implications of tonality, although in varying degrees.

EX. 69

C: V   I   C: I IV   C: VI III   C: VI II   C: IV II
G: I   IV   F: V I   E: IV I   A: I   IV   Bᵇ: V III

The greatest strength of tonality in harmonic progressions involving only triads lies in those progressions which combine dominant harmony with harmony from the subdominant side (including the supertonic as partaking of both). Presence of the tonic chord itself is not necessary to the establishment of a key. More important is the dominant. The progressions IV–V and II–V cannot be interpreted in more than one tonality, without chromatic alteration; hence they do not need the tonic chord to show the key. The progression V–VI, although possible to hear as the relatively uncommon progression I–II in the dominant key, is strongly indicative of a single tonality.

It may be necessary for a third chord to be heard if the harmonic progression is to define the tonality. By adding another chord to the successions in the above example, they can be rendered almost unmistakably in C.

EX. 70

C: IV V I   I IV V   V VI III   VI II V   IV II V

Similarly a third chord could be selected which would confirm the alternative tonality given in the original example.

EX. 71

G: I IV V F: IV V I E: IV I V A: I IV V B♭: V III II

These elementary tonal units, groups of two or three chords with distinct meaning as to key, might be regarded as musical "words." The student is advised to write as many of these formulae as possible in a notebook where they will be available for consultation, beginning with the commonest, like IV–V–I, I–IV–V, etc., and even including some that he may invent. They should then be studied for their individual qualities, their strength of tonality and rhythmic feeling, and notice should be taken of their frequence of use in music and of the varied forms in which they may appear.

Variation of the formulae by differences in doubling, spacing, and choice of soprano note are resources already available to the student.

EX. 72

IV V I   IV V I   IV V I   IV V 1

Change of mode from major to minor, or vice versa, does not affect the tonality of the formula, and it is one of the important means of variation. Ex. 71 could be written as follows, the only change being in the modes.

EX. 73

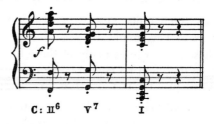

G: I IV V F: IV V I E: IV I V A: I IV V B♭: V III II

The study of harmony deals with the variants of these fundamental formulae, or "words." It will be found that they exist in the
most complex texture, and from the very beginning much attention
should be given to harmonic analysis of standard works, to bring
out the endless capacity for varied treatment of these harmonic
structural elements. Compare these three presentations of the formula
II–V–I:

EX. 74. Mozart—*Sonata, K. 330*

C: II⁶   V⁷   I

EX. 75. Chopin—*Etude, op. 10, no. 6*

E♭: II⁶ᵇ   V⁷   I

EX. 76. Schubert—*Mass no. 6: Kyrie*

E♭: I   IV I   II⁶₅   V⁹₄₂   I

INTERCHANGEABILITY OF THE MODES

The modal implications of the chord progressions have less basic significance than their tonal implications. Major and minor modes are not as distinct in usage as their two scales would seem to indicate, and it is sometimes uncertain which impression is intended by the composer.

Fluctuation between major and minor has always been common.

EX. 77. Beethoven—*Sonata, op. 53*

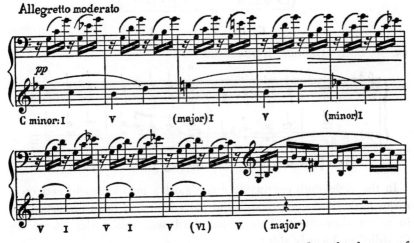

In this example the progression I–V is repeated with change of mode, a change involving but one note—the third degree.

The harmonic progression may itself contain chords from both modes.

EX. 78. Mendelssohn—*Song without Words, op. 102, no. 2*

This use of the sixth degree of the minor mode in the midst of chords of the major mode adds the interest of color and is of fre-

quent occurrence. Both the subdominant and supertonic with minor
sixth degree are freely used when the major is the prevailing mode.

On the other hand, the major forms of these chords (with major
sixth degree) are used in connection with the minor mode only
when the sixth degree ascends to the seventh, according to the
melodic minor scale.

EX. 79

EX. 80. Bach—*Chorale: Herzliebster Jesu*

In the eighteenth century it was almost a mannerism to end on a
major tonic triad even though the movement had been unmistakably
in minor throughout. This major third was called the "tierce de
Picardie" or Picardy third.

EX. 81. Bach—*Well-tempered Clavier, I, Prelude no. 4*

Compositions in large form, of several movements, the first of which
is in the minor mode, more often than not change to major mode
in the last movement, while keeping the same tonality. Beethoven's
Fifth Symphony is always referred to as the C-minor Symphony in

spite of the fact that its final movement is not at all in C minor, but in C major.

The development of chromatic resources in the nineteenth century emphasized the tendency of the two modes to merge into what one is finally tempted to call a chromatic mode. Chromatic tones were introduced partly by the method which has just permitted us to include both A-flat and A-natural in C major, and partly by the extension of the dominant principle to allow other degrees than the tonic to possess their own dominants.

The study of these complexities belongs naturally to an advanced stage in the study of harmony, but there are two points of which the student should be made aware from the start. The first is that the modes, major and minor, tend to become interchangeable, even with triads. Examples from musical literature should be noted and the formulae added to the collection of progressions. In the exercises of the present stage, II and IV can be used with either major or minor sixth degree in the major mode, and the final tonic chord of the minor mode may have a major third. It is understood that these are effects of variety, not to be too regularly introduced.

The second important point is that notes outside the scale do not necessarily affect the tonality. This principle may cause difficulty at first but it should be announced early, if only to emphasize the fact that tonality is established by the progression of roots and the tonal functions of the chords, even though the superstructure of the music may contain all the tones of the chromatic scale.

EXERCISES

Writing some of the exercises without key signature, using accidentals when needed, is helpful for showing the differences in mode and tonality. The traditional signatures of major and minor modes on the same tonic are misleading in that they suggest much more difference than actually exists.

1. Write the modal degrees of the following scales:
    a. A-flat minor
    b. C-sharp major

    c. D-flat major

    d. G-sharp minor

    e. E-flat minor

2. Give the tonalities and modes (major or minor) of the following progressions:

3. Write each of the following harmonic formulae in four different variants, using only triads in root position:

    a. C minor—VI–II–V

    b. E major—II–V–VI

    c. D-flat major—V–VI–IV

    d. A minor—IV–V–I

    e. F major—V–IV–I

4. Write three different four-part versions of each of the following basses, one version in the major mode, one version in the minor mode, and a version using chords from both modes (root position only):

5. Write similar variants of a four-part setting of the following successions of chords, using no key signature (root position only):

    a. Key of G—VI–IV–II–V–III–VI–IV–I–V–I

    b. Key of E-flat—V–I–IV–V–VI–IV–II–V–I–IV–V–I

6. Construct original chord successions, starting with a series of Roman numerals, arranged with attention to the proper distribution of modal and tonal degrees and to the quality of the harmonic progressions involved. The series should finally be worked out in four parts.

Five | CHORDS OF THE SIXTH —THE FIGURED BASS

TRIADS in the first inversion are called chords of the sixth, the characteristic interval being the sixth caused by the inversion of the third.

Adopting the method of musical shorthand widely used by composers in the early eighteenth century, most theorists designate inversions of chords by Arabic numerals showing the intervals made between the bass and the upper voices. Thus a triad in first inversion would be represented by the figures $^6_3$, or simply ^{6}, the third being understood. With Roman numerals identifying the roots, any chord in any inversion can be shown symbolically by this method.

EX. 82

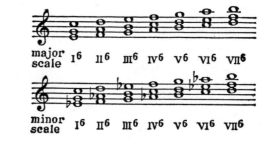

major scale   I⁶   II⁶   III⁶   IV⁶   V⁶   VI⁶   VII⁶

minor scale   I⁶   II⁶   III⁶   IV⁶   V⁶   VI⁶   VII⁶

DOUBLING

In triads in root position the general rule is to double the root, to obtain a fourth tone for four-part writing. This is less generally the rule with triads in first inversion.

The choice of a tone to double is not dependent on whether the triad is major, minor, augmented, or diminished. Nor does it appear to have been, throughout this period of common practice, a question of effective sonority to the ear. The deciding factor is almost invariably the position of the doubled tone in the tonality. In other words, tones are doubled which are important to solidity of the key.

Customary procedure in doubling in chords of the sixth can be stated in these two rules:

a. If the bass (not root) of the chord of the sixth is a tonal degree, it is doubled.

b. If the bass of the chord of the sixth is not a tonal degree, it is not doubled, but a tonal degree in the chord is chosen for doubling.

EX. 83

C: II⁶   D: I⁶

In the above example of the first inversion of a minor triad with D as a root, the F in the first instance is the subdominant, since the key is C. In the second case, the same chord is regarded from the point of view of D minor, in which F is a modal degree, so that either the D, tonic, or A, dominant, is doubled by preference.

GENERAL EFFECT

Harmonically, considered vertically as a sonority, the triad in its first inversion is lighter, less ponderous, less blocklike, than the same triad in root position. It is therefore of value as an element of variety when used with root position chords. Compare the individual sound of the triads in the two versions of a series of triads given below.

EX. 84

A: I   IV   I   II   III   VI   II   V   I

A: I IV⁶   I⁶ II⁶   III⁶ VI   II⁶ V   I

Melodically, the use of chords of the sixth permits the bass to move by step in progressions in which the roots would move by skip. It is difficult to arrange a good melodic line for the bass when the chords are all in root position. The bass will also possess that advantage hitherto allowed only the upper voices, of moving from root to third, and vice versa, in the same harmony.

EX. 85

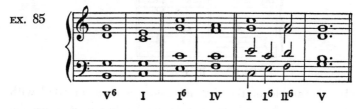

V⁶   I   I⁶   IV   I   I⁶ II⁶   V

Rhythmically, the triad in first inversion is of less weight than one in root position. In the example above, the progressions V₆–I, I₆–IV, and II₆–V are felt as weak-to-strong rhythms, and the I–I₆ as strong-to-weak. The student is reminded, however, that the almost inevitable presence of other factors influencing the rhythm makes it unwise to draw conclusions from a single criterion. In the following example there can be no doubt that the rhythmic stress is on the first beat of the second measure.

EX. 86. Brahms—*Symphony no. 1*

Andante sostenuto

E: I   IV⁶ IV   V⁶   I

VOICE LEADING

There are no new principles of voice leading or of harmonic progression involved in the use of chords of the sixth. The objective of smooth connection of the chords is ever to be kept in mind, the normal progression of the voices being always to the nearest available position. It remains a true principle of contrapuntal practice that doubling and spacing are less important than melodic movement.

EX. 87

G: II   I6   II6   V

Here the stepwise contrary motion in soprano and bass is thought desirable enough to permit the doubling of the modal degree B in the second chord, I6, even though that note has the prominence of being in the outside voices.

CONSECUTIVE CHORDS OF THE SIXTH

When several chords of the sixth occur in succession there is a tendency for the parts to move in similar motion and many examples may be found of the following manner of voice leading:

EX. 88

6   6   6   6   6   6

The direct octaves between tenor and bass can, however, be avoided, and a much more balanced arrangement made:

EX. 89

6   6   6   6 6 6

THE I_6 CHORD

The first inversion of the tonic triad is one of the most useful chords, and at the same time one of the inversions most neglected by the beginner. It serves as a relief from the finality of the tonic triad in root position, and often provides the necessary variety when a chord is needed to follow the dominant. I_6 is a natural harmony to support a melody moving from tonic to dominant by skip.

Some common formulae containing I_6:

EX. 90

$$\text{I}^6 \quad \text{II}^6 \quad \text{V} \quad \text{I} \quad \text{I}^6 \quad \text{IV} \quad \text{V} \quad \text{I}^6 \quad \text{IV} \quad \text{IV} \quad \text{I}^6 \quad \text{V}$$

EX. 91. Beethoven—*Pianoforte Concerto, op. 15*

C: I I^6 II^6 V^7 I

EX. 92. Brahms—*Symphony no. 3*

F: I $\text{II}^6_4 \, (\text{A}^\flat = \text{G}^\sharp)$ I

I⁶(minor)   VI⁶

EX. 93. Mozart—*Sonata, K. 332*

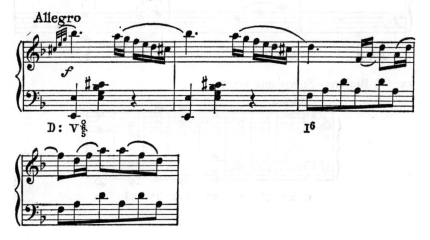

D: V⁶₅   I⁶

THE II₆ CHORD

The supertonic triad in first inversion is very common in cadences, where it precedes and introduces a dominant effect. It is strongly sub-dominant in feeling, the subdominant being the bass tone and usually doubled. II₆ often follows I, whereas II in root position is generally considered an awkward progression from I in root position. In minor, the first inversion is preferred to the root position diminished triad. This minor form is not unusual in combinations with the major tonic triad.

Common formulae:

EX. 94

$$\text{II}^6 \text{ V} \quad \text{I} \quad \text{II}^6 \text{ V} \quad \text{I} \quad \text{I} \quad \text{II}^6 \quad \text{V} \quad \text{VI} \quad \text{II}^6 \quad \text{I}$$

EX. 95. Haydn—*String Quartet, op. 76, no. 4*

$$\text{E}^b\text{: II} \qquad \text{V of II} \quad \text{II}^6 \quad \text{II} \qquad \text{V} \qquad \text{I}$$

EX. 96. Brahms—*Symphony no. 4*

$$\text{E:} \quad \text{II}^6 \quad \text{II}^6 \quad \text{I} \quad \text{II}^6 \quad \text{V of V} \quad \text{I}^6 \quad \text{V}^6_4 \quad \text{I}$$

THE III₆ CHORD

III₆ is not usually an independent chord; it is a good example of the kind of chord made by temporary displacement of one or more tones of some other chord, in this case nearly always the dominant.

EX. 97

In minor it is the inversion of the augmented triad, with its characteristic color. The example below from *Die Walküre* shows this chord actually substituting for a dominant.

Like all other chords of the sixth, it may be found in scalewise passages of weak rhythmic value.

When it proceeds to VI the third degree may be doubled, and regarded temporarily as a dominant of the sixth degree.

Common formulae:

EX. 98

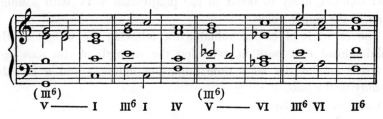

V——— I   III⁶ I   IV   V——— VI   III⁶ VI   II⁶

EX. 99. Brahms—*Sonata for Violin and Piano, op. 108*

D: I   III⁶   VI   I⁶

EX. 100. Wagner—*Die Walküre, Act II*

E: III⁶

EX. 101. Chopin—*Polonaise, op. 40, no. 1*

A: III   II⁶   III⁶ IV⁶   V   I

THE *IV₆* CHORD

The first inversion of the subdominant triad is often used after V. It furnishes a welcome change from VI when the bass moves up by step. This also avoids the cross-relation of the tritone between bass and soprano, likely to occur in the progression V–IV with leading-tone in the upper voice.

The chord is of course valuable for relieving the weight of the subdominant root position, retaining the strength of the root progression and at the same time imparting lightness and a melodic quality to the bass.

Common formulae:

EX. 102

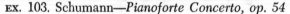

I   V   IV⁶   IV⁶   V   I⁶   I   IV⁶   I⁶

EX. 103. Schumann—*Pianoforte Concerto, op. 54*

A: VofIV₆   IV   VofIV IV⁶   II VofV I⁶₄   V

EX. 104. Brahms—*Song of Fate, op. 54*

Eᵇ: IV⁶   I⁶₄   VofV   V

EX. 105. Beethoven—*Symphony no. 2*

D: I   IV⁶   I⁶ V⁴₃ i   V

THE V₆ CHORD

The third of the dominant is the leading-tone, and the placing of that degree in the bass gives the bass strong melodic significance in addition to lessening the harmonic rigidity of the progression. The bass as leading-tone usually moves to the tonic, so that the next chord will probably be I.

At times the bass may proceed downward, as in a descending scale. In the minor mode this would be the occasion for the use of the descending melodic minor scale in the bass.

Formulae:

EX. 106

I V⁶ I   V⁶   I   I V⁶ IV⁶   I V⁶ IV⁶

EX. 107. Beethoven—*Symphony no. 9*

Adagio

B♭: I   V²   I⁶   V⁶   I V⁶ VI⁷ VofV I⁶₄   V

EX. 108. Mozart—*Overture to Don Giovanni*

D: I

EX. 109. Chopin—*Prelude, op. 28, no. 20*

C: I   VI⁶   V⁶——   IV⁶   II₃⁴   V——

THE VI₆ CHORD

This chord is similar to III₆ in its incapacity to stand as an independent chord. It is nearly always the tonic chord, with the sixth degree as a melodic tone resolving down to the fifth. Usual exceptions to this are found in scalewise progressions of successive chords of the sixth.

Formulae:

EX. 110

I   V   VI⁶ V⁶   I   I   IV⁶

EX. 111. Franck—*Symphony*

D: I ——————

EX. 112. Chopin—*Waltz* (posth.)

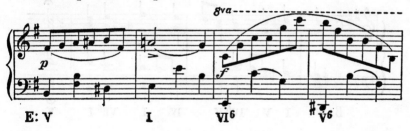

E: V   I   VI⁶   ♯V̊⁶

THE VII₆ CHORD

The leading-tone triad in first inversion is commonly used as a passing chord between the tonic chord in root position and its first inversion. In this case it is rhythmically weak, hardly disturbing the effect of tonic harmony, and it may be analyzed as a grouping of melodic tones above the tonic root. On the other hand, if dwelt upon or otherwise given any prominence, it may be felt as a true dominant harmony, the root V being understood.

In VII₆ the second degree is most often doubled in preference to the more strongly tonal fourth degree, but instances in which the fourth degree is doubled are numerous. (Ex. 115)

Formulae:

EX. 113

I VII⁶ I⁶   IV   VII⁶ I⁶ II⁶   V   I⁶ VII⁶   I
(I ————— IV)

EX. 114. Bach—*Chorale: Ein' feste Burg*

D:I   VI   I   VII⁶ I   VofV V VI   VII⁶ofV I VI⁶ III   IV   VII⁶ I V   I

EX. 115. Bach—*Chorale: Es woll' uns Gott genädig sein*

B: V   I   V   IV⁶ V   IV   I   VII⁶ I   V

EX. 116. Bach—*Well-tempered Clavier, I, Prelude no. 3*

C♯: IV   I⁶   VII⁶   I

EX. 117. Mozart—*Pianoforte Concerto, K. 488*

A: I   VII⁶   I⁶   V of V I⁶⁄₄   V

THE FIGURED BASS

The figured bass had a practical use in the days of Bach and Handel, when the ever-present keyboard instrument required a guide to the harmonic background of the music in order to fill in missing parts or to reinforce weak ones. Today, however, there is no proper place for the *basso continuo,* owing to the standardization of instrumental groupings. Without denying its historical value in the performance of music, one can say that, although it is in general use in the study of harmony, its value as a harmony exercise is rather limited. It is a good shorthand method of designating chords, but the working out of figured basses entails no problem of choosing the appropriate harmony. The problem is solely one of distribution of given materials and of correct voice leading.

Figured basses should be used principally for practice in keyboard harmony. They should preferably not be written out, but played anew each time, taking different soprano notes to start. It is extremely important that they be played rhythmically, even if very slowly.

The principle of denoting upper voices by Arabic numerals permits of prescribing all kinds of melodic tones as well as the chords. The proper method of reading the figures consists in finding the notes by interval and afterwards identifying the resulting chord. The combinations, with practice, get to be as familiar as the notes themselves.

Accidentals are shown by placing the desired signs beside the numerals representing the notes to be affected. An accidental sign standing alone, or under a number, signifies that the third above the bass is to receive that sign. The leading-tone sharp or natural in the minor mode is indicated that way. A line drawn through the numeral has the same meaning as a sharp placed beside it.

The full figuring for a triad in root position would be $\frac{8}{5}$, but this is used only to prescribe the exact doubling. (The order of the voices from the top down need not follow that of the numerals. The figuring is the same whether root, third, or fifth is in the soprano voice.) Root position triads are so common that it is assumed that one is meant when no figure appears. Sometimes just a 5 or a 3 is given to make sure that a triad in root position will be used. For the first inversion, a 6 is sufficient indication, the third being thereby understood.

EXERCISES

1. Write in four parts the following series of chords indicated by symbols:

     a. C minor: III⁶ I IV
     b. G major: I I⁶ IV
     c. A♭ major: III⁶ VI II⁶
     d. A minor: V I⁶ IV
     e. B♭ major: I VII⁶ I⁶
     f. E♭ major: I⁶ II⁶ V
     g. D minor: VI⁶ V⁶ I
     h. B minor: II⁶ V I

i. F major: I V IV⁶

j. D major: II⁶ V I

2. Write out the four-part harmony indicated by the following figured basses:

3. Add three upper voices to the following basses, using chords of the sixth where they are appropriate:

Six | THE HARMONIC
STRUCTURE OF THE
PHRASE

A PHRASE of music seldom contains as many changes of harmony as the average harmony exercise. It may be argued that the purpose of the harmony exercise is to teach the manipulation of chords, and that the more chords it is made to contain the more practice the student will have. But here, as in all other stages of our study, we must continually recall the objective of harmonic theory, namely the clarification of the practice of composers in the use of chords. Harmonized chorales and hymn-tunes, with harmony changing more or less regularly on every beat, represent a very small part of the literature of music in the eighteenth and nineteenth centuries and, however admirable and appropriate to their purpose they may be, they are only partially representative of the common practice of the period.

Just as regularity and symmetry seem to have been sought in rhythm, those qualities are found to be much in evidence when we consider phrase structure. The great majority of phrases, when they have not undergone extension or development, are of four and eight measures. In very slow movement a phrase may contain only two measures and in a fast tempo it may contain sixteen.

Since we are concerned primarily with norms we shall deal at first with four and eight measure phrases. The student will notice, however, the added musical interest of the phrases he finds which do not agree with the standard. These irregular phrases will fall into two categories.

For the most part they will be phrases which were originally four or eight measures long in conception, but have been made longer by one or more technical processes, such as the sequence or the deceptive cadence, harmonic devices to be examined later in this book. The others will have originated with their odd numbers of measures (Ex. 118).

EX. 118. Brahms—*Ballade, op. 118, no. 3*

NUMBER OF HARMONIC CHANGES

It is possible that the phrase be constructed on a static harmony, although there is usually some particular reason for this. Below is an example of a phrase which serves as introduction to the main body of the piece, setting the stage for what is to come. The same phrase is used to close the piece.

EX. 119. Mendelssohn—*Song without Words, op. 62, no. 4*

The other extreme, represented by the following two examples, is very restless in fast tempo but capable of dignity and sturdiness when the movement is rather slow.

EX. 120. Schumann—*Symphonic Studies, op. 13*

Most phrases will show a more balanced harmonic activity. The chord changes are designed to lend life and movement without drawing too much attention to themselves. No rule can be given, as all degrees of variation in the amount of harmonic change can be found between the two extremes.

DISTRIBUTION OF CHORDS

The harmonic rhythm, that is to say, the distribution of chord changes in the phrase, is of great importance in the structure. This principle should be the subject of extensive research during the study of harmony, to bring out the great diversity of effect achieved by harmonic means.

Changes of harmony recurring at regular intervals, like a rhythmic pulse, are fairly common.

EX. 122. Brahms—*Waltz, op. 39, no. 1*

Usually, however, the root changes will form a pattern of harmonic rhythm made up of short and long time values, as well as of weak and strong harmonic progressions.

EX. 123. Beethoven—*Sonata, op. 49, no. 1*

THE PHRASE BEGINNING

Phrases do not necessarily begin with the tonic chord, nor do they necessarily begin on the first beat of a measure. Rhythmically, the start may be either anacrusis (up-beat) or thesis (down-beat). Harmonically, it is customary in the first two or three chords, the first harmonic formula, to make clear the tonality. As has been pointed out, this does not require the presence of the tonic chord.

EX. 124. Mozart—*Sonata, K. 281*

Here the first chord is actually the dominant of C, but, since the key is B-flat and C is the second degree, the chord is properly called V of II, a form of VI.

THE PHRASE ENDING

The end of the phrase is called the cadence, always marked by a certain conventional harmonic formula. It will suffice here to indicate the essential features of two types of cadence, as these will be the object of detailed study in a later chapter.

The *authentic cadence* is comparable to the full stop or period in punctuation, and consists of the progression V–I.

The *half cadence* is like a comma, indicating a partial stop in an unfinished statement. It ends with the chord V, however approached.

The following example shows two phrases, the first ending with a half cadence and the second with an authentic cadence.

EX. 125. Mozart—*Sonata, K. 333*

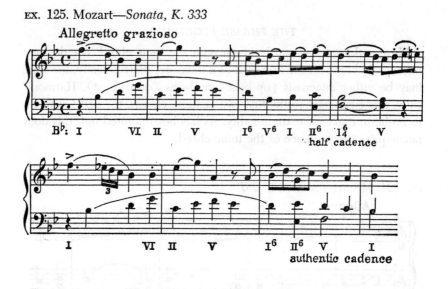

MASCULINE AND FEMININE ENDINGS

Phrase endings are differentiated in harmonic rhythm as to whether they present their final chord as a down-beat or as an up-beat. A cadence having its final chord as a down-beat, usually shown by placing the bar-line just before the final chord, is called a masculine cadence. The example below shows a masculine cadence.

EX. 126. Beethoven—*Violin Concerto, op. 61*

A cadence in which the two final chords give the strong-to-weak, down-up, rhythmic progression is called a feminine cadence, or feminine ending, as in the example below.

EX. 127. Schumann—*Harvest Song, op. 68, no. 24*

UNITY AND VARIETY

The principles governing the selection and distribution of chords within the phrase are those of unity and variety, conditioned by any special purpose for which the phrase is constructed. Such a special purpose is illustrated by Ex. 119, in which the static harmony was appropriate for the introductory function of the phrase. Another special purpose would be that of transition, in which the phrase would be in a state of moving from one place to another, tonally speaking. Another would be the presentation of a phrase previously heard but in a new form, with varied harmony, or with developments and extensions.

Before such aspects are investigated, it is important to know what the harmonic structure consists of in normal phrases having no extraordinary functions, but whose role is simply that of presentation or exposition of the musical thought without development or manipulation.

Harmonically, a phrase consists of a series of harmonic progressions or formulae designed to make clear and maintain the tonality, and to confirm and enhance the harmonic implications in the melodic line. These are principles of unity. The harmony alone will often seem to possess too much unity, with many repetitions of the same root progressions. This is balanced by other significant features in the phrase.

EX. 128. Beethoven—*Sonata, op. 49, no. 2*

(See also Ex. 122.)

Ordinarily, however, it will be found that a great deal of attention has been paid to the matter of balance between unity and variety, both in the choice of roots and in their rhythmic distribution. Investigation of this practice in the works of various composers is extremely profitable.

The more obvious principles of harmonic variety, such as change of key (modulation) and chromatic alteration of the chords, will be subjects for later treatment. The program of study at this point will consist of the following steps:

a. Analysis of a given phrase, deriving a rhythmic pattern of root progressions, shown by Roman numerals.

b. Construction of a four-part harmonic scheme showing the reduction of the original texture to these terms.

c. Using as a basis the pattern obtained in the first step, construction of an original phrase unlike the given phrase.

There follows an illustration of the application of these steps.

EX. 129. Mozart—*Violin Concerto, K. 268*

a. The pattern of root changes is as follows:

EX. 130

The initial up-beat is so comparatively short as to give the impression of anticipating the down-beat with I on the first beat of the first full measure. The I occupies the whole measure. In the second full measure the harmonic rhythm of V–I is short-long, down-up, whereas measure three gives II–V as long-short, proceeding to I on the next down-beat, making a masculine authentic cadence.

b. The original texture can be reduced to the following four-part harmonic scheme:

EX. 131

B♭: I   V   I   II   V   I

c. Taking advantage of the slow tempo to gain variety in the melodic lines by moving about among the chord tones, a version like the one below can be made, using triads in root position and chords of the sixth. Note also the organization of the melodic rhythms.

EX. 132

B♭: I   V   I   II   V   I

EXERCISES

1. Treat the phrases given below, following the three steps as in the example above.

    a. Derive the rhythmic pattern of the roots of the harmony.

    b. Construct the four-part harmonic scheme.

    c. Construct a new phrase from the derived harmonic basis.

Beethoven—*Variations on a Theme by Salieri: Theme*

Handel—*Suite X, Menuetto*

2. Construct original phrases, four measures in length:

   a. Starting with anacrusis and ending with feminine cadence

   b. Starting on thesis and ending with masculine cadence

   c. With minimum of harmonic activity balanced by melodic movement

   d. With maximum of harmonic activity and little melodic movement

3. Construct phrases according to the following patterns:

a. A-flat major, two-four time, slow:

: I V : I V : I V VI II : V :

(*cf.* Beethoven. Sonata Op. 13.)

b. D-major, three-four time, fast:

V : I : V : I : I : V : I II : V :

(*cf.* Beethoven. Sonata Op. 10, no. 3.)

c. A-major, two-four time, slow:

V : I II : V : I IV II : V

(*cf.* Schumann. *In Memoriam from "Album for the Young"* Op. 68, no. 28.)

Seven | HARMONIZATION OF A GIVEN PART

IT must not be thought that the ultimate objective of the study of harmony is the acquisition of the ability to harmonize melodies. That is an accomplishment which ought naturally to come as a by-product of the proper scientific study of harmonic usage, but an accomplishment for which there is a singular lack of opportunity or necessity. Except in restricted, specialized fields, a musician is seldom called upon to furnish harmony for a melody.

The mental steps involved in the process of harmonization make it, however, one of the most valuable exercises in the study of harmony, and it should be regarded always as a means rather than an end. The function of a harmony exercise is to clarify principles by practical experience with the material. The attempt to go over the same ground, to solve the same problems as the composer, will afford, as no purely analytical process can, an insight into the nature and details of these problems and into the manner and variation of their solution.

During the period we are taking as that of harmonic common practice, nearly all the melodies are of harmonic origin. They were either evolved from chord tones, with the addition of nonharmonic melodic tones, or they were conceived as having harmonic meaning, expressed or implied. So the process of harmonization does not mean invention, but in a sense rediscovery of elements already in existence.

Nevertheless, one should discourage the ambition to discover the "author's harmony," especially in academic, manufactured, textbook exercises. There is nothing more depressing than the perusal of the "key to the exercises." Even if the given soprano is a melody by Mozart, no premium should be placed on guessing the exact chords and their arrangement as used by the composer. The profit for the student lies in the intelligent comparison of his own version with that by Mozart.

It is characteristic of the nature of music that any melody is capable of suggesting more than one choice of chords, to say nothing of the numerous possibilities of arranging them. True harmonization, then, means a consideration of the alternatives in available chords, the reasoned selection of one of these alternatives, and the tasteful arrangement of the texture of the added parts with due regard for consistency of style.

ANALYSIS OF THE MELODY

In order to find the available chords for consideration, one should strive to make as complete a harmonic analysis of the melody as possible, in as many versions as seem to present themselves. The first question is, of course, the tonality. Some melodies of restricted range may offer several possibilities of key and mode, even if we limit ourselves to the use of triads in root position.

EX. 133

The possibilities for different interpretations as to tonality and mode of a melodic phrase will increase with the student's further acquaintance with harmonic resources.

Determination of the key will depend upon the diagnosis of the cadence. At present there are but two cadences to be considered, one ending on the dominant chord, and one ending with the progression V–I. In the above example the final note was interpreted in turn as dominant of C, tonic of G, and mediant of E. Tonalities containing one flat or more were not acceptable because of the B-natural in the melody. Likewise keys of two sharps or more were not good since C-natural was present. The absence of the F made it possible to choose keys containing either F-sharp or F-natural. In the E minor version the leading-tone triad was used for the soprano note A, and is here clearly a form of dominant harmony.

Having decided on the key and having marked the Roman numerals of the last two chords, one should next consider the frequency of change of the harmony. With triads in root position there will not be a great deal of flexibility in this, but two opportunities may be offered for departure from the monotonous regularity of one chord for each soprano note.

MELODIC SKIPS

When a melody moves by skip, it is likely that the best procedure will be to use the same harmony for both notes.

EX. 134

G: I ——————— V

Exceptions to this will usually arise from questions of harmonic rhythm. If the two notes involved in the skip occur at a point where the harmonic rhythm would appropriately move from weak to strong, then the harmonic roots will probably be different.

EX. 135

G: I V VI IV I V

Such a rhythmic effect is generally placed so that the second chord falls on the first beat of a measure, giving rise to the often stated rule that it is better to change root over a bar-line. The weak-to-strong rhythm may, however, be found within the measure, just as the first beat, as we have seen, is sometimes not the strongest.

EX. 136

G: I V VI IV I V

SUSTAINED TONES

If the harmonic rhythm seems to demand frequent chord changes, it may happen that a tone of the melody will hold through as a tone common to two or more different chords.

EX. 137

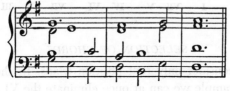

G: I VI IV V III VI V

It is, of course, possible that melodic movement in the other voices, without change of root, may be more desirable.

EX. 138

G: IV V I V

AVAILABLE CHORDS

After having decided on the tonality and having made a prelimi-
nary decision as to the general harmonic activity, or frequency of
chords, each note of the given part should be examined for its possibilities as a chord tone. These should actually be written, as Roman
numerals, in order that all the mental steps may be clearly seen.

In working with a given bass only one chord was available for each
tone, since the given bass notes were at the same time the roots of the
triads. When an upper voice is given, each tone furnishes a choice of
three triads. A given tone can be the root, the third, or the fifth.

EX. 139

This step is shown applied to a short melodic soprano part:

EX. 140

SELECTION OF CHORDS

Let us first consider only root position triads. In the last measure
of the above example we can at once eliminate the VI and the IV, as
we wish to end the phrase with either V or I. Since I remains, the
cadence will be an authentic cadence, so we choose V to precede the
I. The VII would not be a good substitute for V here because it would
give a doubled leading-tone. In measure 4 we can also eliminate the
VII in favor of the stronger IV or II. In measure 3 either I or VI
could serve for the whole measure. In measure 2 the VII's can be
struck out, since they would lose their identity if associated with the
V. Also the II will prove a troublesome choice for the second beat as

it would make parallel octaves if followed by I, and would not give
a very satisfactory bass interval if followed by VI. So we conclude
that measure 2 had better contain either IV–V or II–V. These elimi-
nations leave the following alternatives:

EX. 141

Considering what we now have from the standpoint of unity and
variety, and harmonic rhythm, we see that the only chance to use VI
is in measure 3, and that the progression V–VI would be good here as
a variation to the V–I which must come at the end. So we eliminate
the I, and in consequence decide that we had better use I in the first
measure for unity. In measure 4 both IV and II could be included
under the same soprano note, adding variety of melodic and harmonic
rhythm, in which case we would not use II in measure 5, but keep
V for the whole measure.

The above reasoning brings us to the conclusion below, with the
resultant bass part. It is obviously not the only conclusion possible
but the bass appears to be a good one. Comparison of the two melodic
curves shows a good amount of contrary motion, a quality to be sought
between soprano and bass.

EX. 142

Writing the inside parts will often require irregularities of doubling
and changes of position. Care should be taken to make the connections
as smooth as possible and to avoid parallel octaves and fifths.

EX. 143

The above are mental steps in the reconstruction of the harmonic background of a given melodic part. It is inadvisable to hurry over them or to omit them in favor of a harmonization which happens to present itself spontaneously, especially in the first stages of study. The weighing of the pros and cons, so to speak, of each problem of detail and of the whole constitutes a profitable experience and practice which even the person gifted with a flair for improvisatory harmonization cannot afford to miss.

DIVISION INTO PHRASES

The melody will probably contain more than one phrase, unless it is a single phrase purposely designed for practice, or isolated from its surroundings. The problem of the location of the cadences is very often simplified by an obvious break or resting point in the course of the line.

EX. 144

In other cases there may be less evidence in the melody itself, or even an ambiguity, so that it becomes a function of the harmony to make clear the punctuation of the phrases by the presence of a cadential formula, preferably a half cadence, sometimes reinforced by the arrangement of the harmonic rhythm.

EX. 145

half cadence ——⌐
V

Here it would be possible to follow what at first sight seems to be the phraseology suggested by the melody, ending the phrase on the half-note G. A more satisfactory balance is obtained, however, by a half cadence in which the dominant harmony occupies the whole of the fourth measure. The half-note G would then be the start of the second phrase.

USE OF FORMULAE

It was advocated in the course of the discussion of tonality that groups of two or three chords might be learned as commonly recurring formulae or harmonic words. A vocabulary of such words is extremely useful in the planning of a harmonization. One recognizes an upper voice of one of the formulae as part of the melody and the stage of considering alternate chords becomes a stage of considering alternate formulae.

EX. 146

This group of notes, or motive, instead of being regarded as four isolated chord tones to be related, could be remembered as the familiar upper voice of a number of formulae, such as these:

EX. 147

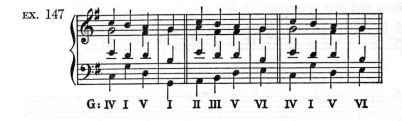

G: IV I V   I   II III V   VI   IV I   V   VI

Or, if chords of the sixth are included:

EX. 148

G: IV III⁶ V VI IV⁶ I VII⁶ I⁶ VII⁶ I⁶ II⁶ VI

The principles of unity and variety are noticeable in a good harmonization. The harmony does not go so far afield as to be irrelevant to the intentions of the melody, but it is desirable that it should at some moment present some aspect which is not entirely commonplace and expected. The bass should be a good contrapuntal line in comparison with the given part. The harmonic rhythm should be planned to corroborate the fundamental pulse implied by the melody and to add rhythmic interest at points where this is not contributed by the given voice. The rhythmic and melodic style of all the added parts should be in accord with the style of the given part.

EXERCISES

In addition to the written exercises designed to apply the points raised by each chapter, it is expected that students will be given much practical harmonic analysis as a parallel activity. One class meeting per week devoted to the analysis of works important in the development of harmony in the eighteenth and nineteenth centuries is not excessive.

1. Harmonize the following soprano melodies, using triads in root position and first inversion.

2. Add three upper voices to the following basses.

Eight | NONHARMONIC TONES

ITᴛ is noticeable that the texture of music contains melodic tones which are not members of the chord against which they are sounded. Literally, there is no such thing as a nonharmonic tone, since tones sounding together create harmony. We know this process to be the very origin of chords. But the language of music has grown like any other language. Certain forms become established through usage. We sense a harmonic background capable of reduction to a comparatively small number of chords which we call the harmonic material of music. These chords make up the harmonic scheme we have been drawing up to represent the skeleton, or framework, upon which the more complex melodic structure rests, and, as we have seen, they contribute their own underlying rhythmic life to the whole.

The contrapuntal material of music comprises all the melodic tones and rhythms which are interwoven to make the texture. Some of these tones appear as factors of the chords and some do not. Those that do not are customarily called nonharmonic tones.

It is important to understand that the nonharmonic tones do not derive their melodic and rhythmic characteristics from the fact that they are foreign to the harmony. Their true nature is inherently melodic and can be discovered by study of the melodic line alone. The purely melodic quality is emphasized by their not agreeing with the chord tones, but it frequently happens that one of these tones is identical with a chord tone.

EX. 149

The E in the tenor is a chord tone, while that in the soprano is a melodic decoration of the resolution to C of the suspended D.

The implied anachronism in the accepted term "nonharmonic tones" may be excused on the ground that during the period of harmonic common practice, which we are studying, the composers were so chord-minded that it may be assumed they created melody by reference to harmony. In this way the tones would more readily be divided into those which are chord tones and those which are not. This is the point of view recommended in the study of harmony, leaving the other more historical aspects to the study of counterpoint and melodic analysis. Neither is complete in itself as a description of the practice of composers.

THE PASSING TONE

A melodic skip may be filled in with tones on all intervening steps, either diatonic or chromatic. These are called passing tones.

EX. 150

The interval filled in by passing tones is not necessarily an interval between two members of the same chord.

EX. 151

Passing tones are rhythmically weak, and may occur on any beat or fraction of the measure. They are not accented. The "accented passing tone" is really an appoggiatura. In the example below it is obvious that the passing tones are unaccented even though taking place on the beat.

EX. 152. Beethoven—*Sonata, op. 10, no. 3*

The composer may cause a passing tone to be accented by the use of dynamic signs, calling for an accentuation which otherwise would not occur.

EX. 153. Mozart—*String Quartet, K. 387*

Passing tones are employed in all voices, and when used simultaneously in different voices may result in a degree of complexity. Too many such tones tend to obscure the underlying framework and weaken the effect of the music. The student is advised to study the works of Sebastian Bach as models of balance in the use of all non-harmonic tones. In applying these resources in exercises it is recommended that they be sparingly used at first, allowing the emphasis to fall on clarity of harmonic structure.

EX. 154. Bach—*Chorale: Jesu, der du meine Seele*

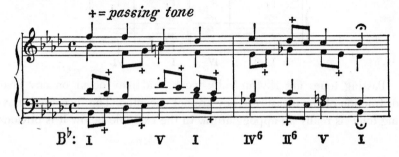

EX. 155. Bach—*Well-tempered Clavier, II, Fugue no. 17*

+ = passing tone

A♭: V   I⁶ VI V⁷ofV   V⁷. V⁷ofIV———IV   V I V⁶ III

In the minor mode, the sixth and seventh degrees, when they are used as passing tones, will be derived from the melodic scale, ascending or descending.

EX. 156

pt. pt.

C: I   V   pt.   I

THE AUXILIARY TONE

The auxiliary tone (also called embellishment, neighboring note, *broderie*) is a tone of weak rhythmic value which serves to ornament a stationary tone. It is approached by either a half or a whole step from the tone it ornaments and it returns to that tone.

EX. 157

EX. 158. Bach—*Brandenburg Concerto no. 3*

Allegro x = auxiliary

A change of harmony may take place as the auxiliary returns to the main tone.

EX. 159. Chopin—*Prelude, op. 28, no. 4*

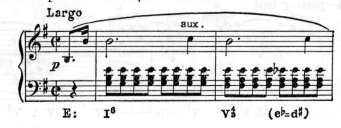

The auxiliary tone is not always a scale degree of the key, but is frequently altered chromatically to bring it a half-tone closer to the main tone. When it is below, it has the character of a temporary leading-tone of the scale degree it attends.

EX. 160. Mozart—*Sonata, K. 331*

The upper and lower auxiliaries combine to form a melodic turn of five notes around a central tone.

EX. 161. Schumann—*Carnaval, op. 9*

The melodic figure shown above is often found with the third note omitted. Various names have been given to this grouping, but we shall refer to it as the double auxiliary, implying that it is a single tone ornamented by two auxiliary tones.

EX. 162. Berlioz—*Fantastic Symphony*

Two or three auxiliaries occurring at the same time in similar motion make a chord which might be termed an auxiliary chord.

EX. 163. Liszt—*Les Préludes*

THE APPOGGIATURA

All nonharmonic tones are rhythmically weak, with the single exception of the appoggiatura (pl. appoggiature). The derivation of the term (from the Italian verb *appoggiare*, to lean) gives the best clue to its character. It gives the impression of leaning heavily on the tone into which it finally resolves, by half or whole step. The rhythm of the appoggiatura followed by its note of resolution is invariably strong-to-weak.

In arranging an appoggiatura with a four-part chord, it is customary to avoid doubling the note of resolution, especially when the appoggiatura is not in the upper voice. The note of resolution is doubled in the bass in chords in root position, the appoggiatura being far enough above to be clearly followed melodically.

EX. 164

EX. 165. Beethoven—*Sonata, op. 7*

The appoggiatura may be below the note toward which it is tending. Commonest of this type is the leading-tone appoggiatura to the tonic.

EX. 166. Haydn—*Sonata*

Like the auxiliary, the appoggiatura is often found as a chromatically altered scale degree. The alteration gives it an added tendency toward its destination similar to the tendency of a leading-tone.

EX. 167. Brahms—*Pianoforte Concerto, op. 83*

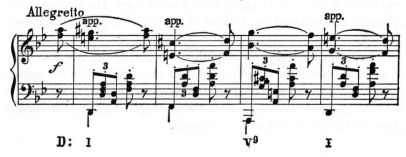

A most pungent form of appoggiatura is that of the lowered seventh degree, descending minor, standing for the sixth degree and sounding against the leading-tone in dominant harmony. This creates the somewhat unusual interval of the diminished octave.

EX. 168. Bizet—*L'Arlésienne*

Several appoggiature sounding together make an appoggiatura chord.

EX. 169. Chopin—*Prelude, op. 28, no. 6*

THE SUSPENSION

The suspension is a tone whose natural progression has been rhythmically delayed.

EX. 170

It is interesting to note that the melodic rhythm of the voice containing the suspension is strong-to-weak, long-to-short, while the harmonic rhythm is felt here as weak-to-strong. If the C were not tied over, the effect would be of an appoggiatura and the melodic rhythm would then agree with the harmonic rhythm.

EX. 171

The tied note is characteristic of the suspension, as this is the means
by which the note is delayed while the root changes.

EX. 172. Schumann—*Romance, op. 28*

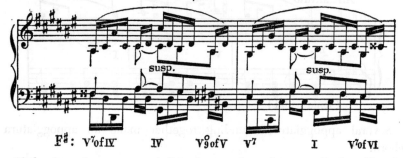

F♯: V⁷ofIV   IV   V⁹₉ofV   V⁷   I   V⁷ofVI

If the first of two notes tied is shorter than the second, the effect is
rather of an appoggiatura anticipated, or arriving too early.

EX. 173. Scarlatti—*Sonata*

G: I   V   V⁷ofIV   IV   V⁷ofIII

The resolution of the suspension is usually to the scale step below,
but the upward resolution is not infrequent. If the suspended note
is a leading-tone, or chromatically raised tone, it will have a natural
resolution to the note above.

EX. 174. Beethoven—*String Trio, op. 3*

E♭: V⁴₃   I   VofII   II   VofIII   III

When several tones are suspended at once they will constitute a suspended chord, so that there may be two harmonies heard at the same time, a familiar effect in cadences of slow movements.

EX. 175. Brahms—*Intermezzo, op. 116, no. 6*

ORNAMENTAL RESOLUTION

In normal rhythmic movement the amount of time a tone is suspended is at least the value of one whole beat or pulse. The suspension does not usually resolve on a fraction of a beat, especially the second half of the first beat. There are, however, a number of ornamental resolutions of the suspension which may provide melodic activity before the actual note of resolution arrives. These ornamental resolutions may occur in the form of auxiliary, échappée, cambiata (pl. cambiate), or anticipation (see below), or there may be a chord tone interpolated between the suspension and its resolution.

EX. 176

EX. 177. Handel—*Suite no. 3*

ÉCHAPPÉE AND CAMBIATA

The melodic forms described above in the ornamental resolution of the suspension are applied to any basic melodic progression of a second, up or down. The commonest use of the échappée, as well as of the cambiata, is as an interpolated tone between a dissonant tone, or tendency tone, and its resolution. The échappée is like a note escaping from the direction of the melodic movement and having to return by skip, that is, by an interval larger than a second. On the other hand, the cambiata is the result of having gone too far, so that it is necessary to turn back by step to the note of destination.

EX. 178

a

melodic movement   échappée   cambiata

b

melodic movement   échappée   cambiata

EX. 179. Haydn—*String Quartet, op. 76, no. 3*

EX. 180. Brahms—*Variations on a Theme by Haydn*

EX. 181. Mozart—*Sonata, K. 533*

EX. 182. Chopin—*Mazurka, op. 59, no. 2*

THE ANTICIPATION

As its name implies, the anticipation is a kind of advance sounding of a note. It is rhythmically like an up-beat to the tone anticipated, to which it is usually not tied, and it is ordinarily much shorter in time value than the principal tone.

EX. 183. Franck—*String Quartet*

EX. 184. Handel—*Concerto Grosso*

APPLICATION

The practical application of the principles of nonharmonic tones
will involve two different processes, one analytical and one constructive. The first will be called into play in the practice of harmonizing
a given part. It will be necessary to devote much thought in the
melodic analysis to deciding which are essential notes and which are
nonharmonic tones. The experience of harmonic analysis of compositions will prove helpful in this respect.

It is recommended that the constructive process be based on the
hypothesis of the harmonic background as the origin of melodic parts.
The steps would be as follows:

1. Adopt a tonality and sequence of roots as a foundation for a
musical sentence. Let us take for example: B-flat major, I–IV–II–V–
I–V, III–IV–I–II–III–V–I.

2. Construct a bass by applying to the above series the principles
of harmonic rhythm, using triads in root position and first inversion.

EX. 185

3. Add three upper voices in a fairly simple version of this harmonic scheme.

EX. 186

4. Apply the various resources of nonharmonic tones to ornament the four voices, without destroying their fundamental melodic progression. This step is practically without limit as to possible variants, although it is useless to strive for complexity.

EX. 187

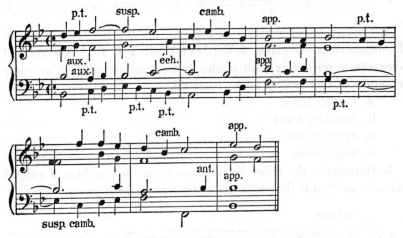

EXERCISES

1. Harmonize the following soprano parts, observing the nonharmonic tones indicated. Other nonharmonic tones may be introduced in the added voices.

2. Construct four versions of a phrase on the following series of harmonic roots: G major, I–V–III–VI–IV–II–V–I. Each version will concentrate on one type of nonharmonic tone, introducing as many examples of that type as seems practical.

    a. Passing tones

    b. Auxiliary tones

    c. Appoggiature

    d. Suspensions

3. Harmonize the following soprano parts, first making a careful melodic analysis to determine the nonharmonic tones present.

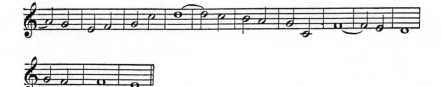

4. Harmonize the following basses. Note that the triads are not necessarily in root position.

Nine | THE SIX-FOUR CHORD

WHEN a triad is so arranged that its original fifth is the lowest tone (second inversion), the resulting combination is known as the six-four chord, the intervals between bass and upper voices being sixth and fourth.

EX. 188

Since the fourth is a dissonant interval when its lowest tone is the bass, and the sixth but an imperfect consonance, the six-four chord is an unstable chord. It is normally the product of vertical coincidence of moving voices. When correctly used it can be analyzed as a grouping of nonharmonic tones.

THE CADENTIAL SIX-FOUR CHORD

By far the commonest of the chords in this category is the familiar "tonic six-four" found in cadences. This is actually a dominant chord in which the sixth and fourth form appoggiature to the fifth and third respectively.

EX. 189

In four-part writing the bass of the cadential six-four chord is doubled, since it is the inactive tone, and also since it is the real root of a dominant chord in root position.

It will be profitable to compare the above formula with the following closely related effects.

EX. 190

The cadential six-four chord, with its resolution to the dominant chord, has the rhythmic value of strong-to-weak. In its most characteristic form it marks a strong down-beat, and the bar-line is most often placed just before it. The harmony preceding the cadential six-four chord is one that would introduce the dominant by means of a weak-to-strong progression, for example, IV–V, II–V, or even I–V.

EX. 191

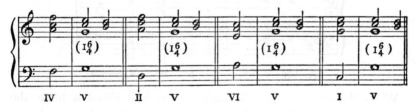

EX. 192. Wagner—*Die Meistersinger, Act I, Chorale*

It must be remembered, however, that the placing of the bar-lines, representing the meter, may be often at variance with the harmonic and melodic rhythms. The six-four chords in the two examples below occur on what are felt to be strong beats, not necessarily first beats of the measures. Not only does the longer time value of the dominant harmony give it rhythmic weight, but the down-beat feeling of the two appoggiature, the sixth and the fourth, contributes melodically to the effect. But this effect of strong-weak, down-up, concerns only the I_4^6–V cadential progression itself. In terms of the rhythmic sense of the whole phrase the dominant harmony, represented by I_4^6–V, gives, in these two excerpts, a good example of a strong up-beat.

EX. 193. Beethoven—*Sonata, op. 2, no. 2*

EX. 194. Mozart—*Sonata, K. 331*

When the chord before the cadential six-four chord is tonic, the progression is nevertheless felt as weak-to-strong, since the root change is actually I–V.

EX. 195. Beethoven—*String Quartet, op. 18, no. 2*

Adagio cantabile

Chords on III and V are less appropriate to introduce the cadential six-four chord, as the resulting harmonic rhythm is either strong-to-weak or static.

EX. 196

The sixth or the fourth, or both, may occur as suspensions, tied over from the previous beat, instead of as appoggiature. In this case the harmonic rhythm remains weak-to-strong, while the melodic rhythm of the two voices involved becomes strong-to-weak.

EX. 197

In the next example, the chord on the first beat of the second measure could be described as a supertonic six-four chord, but the sixth is a suspension and the fourth an appoggiatura, so that the basic harmony of the first two beats is really VI.

EX. 198. Mozart—*Pianoforte Quartet, K. 478*

The sixth and fourth, although they are by origin nonharmonic tones, may function as principal melodic tones with further embellishment. Thus the E in the second measure of the example below, the sixth of the chord, is decorated by the appoggiatura F-sharp and the auxiliary D-sharp.

EX. 199. Brahms—*Intermezzo, op. 117, no. 3*

In keeping with the contrapuntal character of the sixth and fourth, care is taken, as a rule, to observe their natural resolution to the step below. The following resolutions are exceptional.

EX. 200

EX. 201. Mozart—*String Quartet, K. 421*

Other harmonies may be interpolated between the six-four chord and its resolution to the dominant. The quality of suspense inherent in the cadential six-four chord is retained by the ear until the dominant is reached.

EX. 202. Bach—*Chorale: Jesu, nun sei gepreiset*

EX. 203. Chopin—*Mazurka, op. 50, no. 3*

This effect of suspense is carried to the extreme in long, developed, concerto cadenzas, which are inserted between the cadential six-four chord and the expected dominant.

THE APPOGGIATURA SIX-FOUR CHORD—NONCADENTIAL

Although found chiefly in cadences, the six-four chord formed from the notes of the tonic triad may be used as a strong rhythmic effect elsewhere in the phrase. The cadential impression will not be likely if such a chord occurs early in the phrase and it may be avoided by melodic continuity in the voices.

EX. 204

Analogous chords are used on other degrees of the scale, the combination IV_4^6–I being fairly common.

EX. 205. Weber—*Sonata, op. 49*

$$B^\flat\text{: } I \underline{\hspace{2cm}} (IV^6_4) \qquad I$$

EX. 206. Schubert—*Sonata, op. 53*

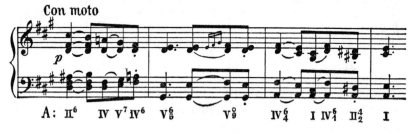

$$A\text{: } II^6 \quad IV\ V^7\ IV^6 \quad V^6_5 \qquad V^o_9 \qquad IV^6_4 \quad I\ IV^6_4 \quad II^4_2 \quad I$$

THE AUXILIARY SIX-FOUR CHORD

If the root of a triad remains stationary while its third and fifth rise one degree and return, a six-four chord is formed. This type differs from the appoggiatura type in that it is weak rhythmically and the sixth and fourth must enter from below in the manner of auxiliary tones. A simple analysis of one root for all three chords is always possible, the sixth and fourth being nonharmonic tones.

EX. 207

EX. 208. Beethoven—*Six Variations, op. 34*

$$F\text{: } I \quad IV^6_4\ I \quad \overset{V^7}{/I} \quad I \qquad I\ V\text{of}IV\ IV^6\ V^6_5\ I \quad I^6_4 \qquad V$$

THE PASSING SIX-FOUR CHORD

It is the bass, rather than the upper voices, that gives its name to the passing six-four chord. Here the bass is a passing tone between two tones a third apart, usually of the same harmony. The rhythmic value of the passing six-four chord is therefore weak. Its upper voices enter and leave by step, so that they may be explained contrapuntally in relation to the surrounding harmony, the sixth as auxiliary, the fourth as harmony note, and the octave of the bass as passing tone.

EX. 209

EX. 210. Mozart—*Sonata, K. 330*

EX. 211. Brahms—*Pianoforte Concerto, op. 83*

In the following example of the passing six-four chord, the two inner parts remain stationary while bass and soprano proceed as passing tones.

EX. 212. Mendelssohn—*Song without Words, op. 85, no. 4*

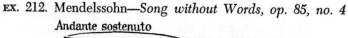

The bass may touch upon the fifth in the course of its melodic movement among the tones of the chord, without producing the dissonant effect of a six-four chord. It must be decided on rhythmic grounds whether or not the fifth is the real harmonic bass. Certainly in the example below the fifth in the bass is unimportant contrapuntally and is merely a tone in a broken chord.

EX. 213. Mozart—*String Quartet, K. 465*

Six-four chords of contrapuntal origin are frequent and can be understood as groupings of any of the nonharmonic tones. They are usually not of sufficient rhythmic importance to be looked upon as chords, but rather should be regarded as combinations of melodic factors.

EX. 214

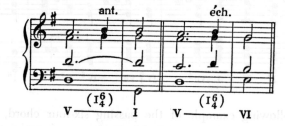

Composers have occasionally been attracted by the feeling of suspense in the six-four chord and have used it for that effect. Schumann

preferred to end the Romance in F-sharp that way rather than with the finality of a root position tonic chord.

EX. 215. Schumann—*Romance, op. 28, no. 2*

F#: I   V   I⁶₄ ⎯⎯⎯⎯⎯⎯⎯

Common formulae including six-four chords, to be played in all keys:

EXERCISES

1. Write in four parts the following series of chords indicated by symbols:

> a. A minor: VI II⁶ I⁶₄ V
> b. B♭ major: II I⁶₄ V I
> c. G minor: V VI I⁶₄ V
> d. E major: V I⁶₄ V VI
> e. C minor: I V⁶₄ I⁶ V
> f. D major: IV⁶₄ I I⁶₄ V
> g. B minor: I I⁶₄ II⁶ V
> h. F major: I⁶₄ III⁶ IV I

2. Work out the following figured basses in four parts:

3. Harmonize the following soprano parts, introducing six-four chords where appropriate:

4. Harmonize the following basses:

$\mathcal{T}en$ | CADENCES

THERE are no more important formulae than those used for phrase endings. They mark the breathing places in the music, establish the tonality, and render coherent the formal structure.

It is remarkable that the convention of the cadential formulae could hold its validity and meaning throughout the entire period of common harmonic practice. The changes that took place in external manner, in harmonic color, did not disturb the fundamental cadence types, but seemed only to serve to confirm their acceptance.

THE AUTHENTIC CADENCE

The harmonic formula V–I, the authentic cadence, can be extended to include the II or IV which customarily precede. We now have the cadential six-four chord, whose natural function is to announce the cadence. The strongest form of final cadence would then be II_6–I_4^6–V–I. The tonic six-four chord is, of course, the double appoggiatura on the dominant root.

EX. 216. Bach—*Well-tempered Clavier, II, Fugue no. 9*

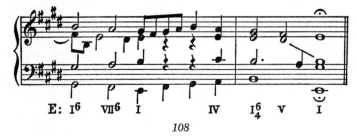

The example above shows the strength and finality of this cadence in simple form. There are many ways of varying the arrangement of the formula. The six-four chord may not be present, and the fourth alone may appear as a suspension.

EX. 217. Handel—*Suite no. 6*

The final tonic chord may receive some ornamentation, such as a suspension or an appoggiatura.

EX. 218. Tchaikowsky—*Romance, op. 5*

The dominant chord may continue to sound over the final tonic in the bass, later resolving, or it may act as an appoggiatura chord to the tonic.

EX. 219. Franck—*Sonata for Violin and Piano*

PERFECT AND IMPERFECT CADENCES

The use of the authentic cadence is not restricted to final phrases. It is often employed elsewhere, but with less emphasis on its finality. The most conclusive arrangement, with dominant and tonic chords in root position and the tonic note in the soprano at the end, is generally called the perfect cadence, all other forms of the authentic cadence being termed imperfect, meaning less final.

A hard and fast distinction between what are perfect and what are imperfect cadences is not possible, nor is it important. The degree of finality is dependent upon many contributing factors and each case should be judged on its own merits.

The approach to the tonic by means of the first inversion of the dominant chord is generally considered a less conclusive cadential effect.

EX. 220. Mendelssohn—*Prelude, op. 25, no. 6*

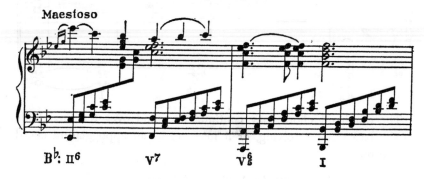

If the tonic chord itself is inverted the phrase will probably be extended so that the real cadence comes later. Placing the third in the soprano usually gives less feeling of finality than having the tonic in both outside voices. The following example by Beethoven shows an imperfect authentic cadence, with third in soprano and feminine ending, balanced by a perfect cadence with masculine ending and tonic in soprano and bass.

EX. 221. Beethoven—*Symphony no. 8*

THE HALF CADENCE

EX. 222. Bach—Chorale: *Aus meines Herzens Grunde*

The cadential six-four chord is also employed to accentuate the half cadence, common formulae being IV–I$_4^6$–V, II–I$_4^6$–V, VI–I$_4^6$–V, I–I$_4^6$–V.

EX. 223

EX. 224. Mozart—*Sonata, K. 576*

The tonic may be suspended into the dominant chord, without six-four, or may appear as appoggiatura to the leading-tone.

EX. 225. Brahms—*Intermezzo, op. 117, no. 2*

In many cases the chord before the dominant will contain a chromatically raised fourth degree, making a leading-tone to the dominant. This has more melodic than harmonic significance, as illustrated by the cambiata G-sharp in the example below.

EX. 226. Beethoven—*Sonata, op. 2, no. 2*

This temporary leading-tone may, however, be of sufficient harmonic strength to give the chord the character of dominant of the dominant (VofV). As such it is also used as an appoggiatura chord over the dominant root.

EX. 227. Schubert—*Quintet, op. 163*

It is not essential to differentiate between a half cadence containing the chord VofV and an authentic cadence in the key of the dominant. When the subsequent phrase is still in the tonic key it seems useless to consider that there is a modulation just on account of one chord. On the other hand, if there is a strong series of chords in the dominant key leading up to the cadence it would appear more logical to recognize a modulation in the analysis.

THE PLAGAL CADENCE

The plagal cadence (IV–I) is most often used after an authentic cadence, as a sort of added close to a movement. The subdominant chord seems tonally very satisfactory after the emphasis on dominant and tonic.

EX. 228. Chopin—*Etude, op. 25, no. 8*

There are many instances of the plagal cadence as a phrase ending, without a preceding authentic cadence.

EX. 229. Schumann—*Symphonic Studies, op. 13*

C♯: Vof IV   IV   Vof IV IV   I

The minor form of subdominant harmony is frequently used in the plagal cadence at the end of a movement in the major mode. It gives a particularly colorful ending.

EX. 230. Mendelssohn—*Midsummer Night's Dream: Overture*

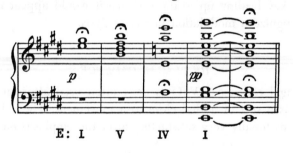

E: I   V   IV   I

The supertonic may be added to the subdominant chord without impairing the effect of plagal cadence. It may appear as a passing tone or it may be a chord tone in a seventh chord in first inversion. Used in this way, the II $^6_5$ is regarded as a substitute for IV.

IV   I   II$^6_5$ I

EX. 232. Brahms—*Symphony no. 1*

THE DECEPTIVE CADENCE

There remains the fourth type of cadential formula, the deceptive cadence. It is similar to the authentic cadence except that some other chord is substituted for the final tonic. There are as many deceptive cadences as there are chords to which the dominant may progress, plus the variations in arrangement which composers have devised. Needless to say, some are more "deceptive" than others and some will seem overworked.

The deceptive cadence is quite as good an indicator of the tonality as the other cadences—often even better. It is the establishment of the dominant as such which shows the key, and not its ultimate chord of resolution. The identification of the cadential formula is the means of identifying the tonality of the phrase.

By far the most frequent alternative to V–I is V–VI. In the example below, the dominant chord appears as appoggiatura chord over the sixth degree.

EX. 233. Schubert—*Sonata, op. 120*

If the minor sixth degree is used for the submediant chord, in a phrase which has been predominantly major, there is more of the element of surprise in the resolution. Composers sometimes accentuate this effect, as in other deceptive cadences, by a sudden change of nuance or of orchestration.

EX. 234. Schubert—*String Quartet, op. 29*

Between the V and the VI the dominant harmony of the sixth degree may be used as a passing chord. This does not change the main outline of the cadence or the tonality.

EX. 235. Beethoven—*Sonata, op. 101*

Upon the same bass as the V–VI cadence, the chord of resolution may be the subdominant in first inversion. In the following example the appoggiatura B-flat adds to the effectiveness of the deceptive cadence, which is here especially strong as it has been led up to with every musical and psychological appearance of a conclusive ending of the entire prelude.

EX. 236. Bach—*Well-tempered Clavier, I, Prelude no. 8*

Bach has introduced still another deceptive cadence in the same piece, after that shown above. This time the dominant resolves to a tonic chord which has been altered to make it a dominant of the subdominant.

EX. 237. Bach—*Well-tempered Clavier, I, Prelude no. 8*

Dominants of other degrees of the scale and other chromatically altered chords may be found in the deceptive cadence. The example below shows a seventh chord on the sixth degree with its root and third raised. If allowed to resolve in the key this chord would proceed to V.

EX. 238. Brahms—*Intermezzo, op. 116, no. 6*

As can be seen in several of these examples, the deceptive cadence often serves as a joint between two overlapping phrases. Phrases are overlapping when the second phrase begins simultaneously with the arrival of the last chord of the first phrase. Overlapping phrases are to be seen in examples 234, 236, and 237.

Phrases which are not overlapping may seem so on first sight, owing to melodic continuity in the final measure of the first phrase. In this case the melodic movement over the last chord in the cadence is in the form of anacrusis to the first down-beat in the second phrase. This frequently happens in the half cadence.

EX. 239. Mozart—*Rondo, K. 485*

The use of a deceptive cadence near the end of a piece helps to sustain the musical interest at the moment when the final authentic cadence is expected. It also provides the composer with an opportunity to add another phrase or two in conclusion.

Cadences are sometimes extended by repetition of the cadential formula, or by lengthening the time values of the harmonic rhythm while continuing the melodic activity above.

EX. 240. Bach—*Well-tempered Clavier, I, Fugue no. 4*

Cadential formulae, to be played in all keys:

EXERCISES

1. Write in four parts the following series of chords indicated by symbols. Each short phrase should be given rhythmic organization, with bar-lines showing the meter chosen. Introduce nonharmonic tones.

    a. E♭ major: VII⁶ I I⁶ IV I⁶₄ V I
    b. D minor: I VI IV II V I
    c. G major: I⁶ IV V VI II I⁶₄ V
    d. A minor: V⁶ I IV II I⁶₄ V VI
    e. D major: I VII⁶ I⁶ IV I⁶₄ V I
    f. F♯ minor: II V VI II V I IV I

2. Work out the following figured basses in four parts:

3. Harmonize the following unfigured basses:

Moderato

a

Andante

b

Moderato

c

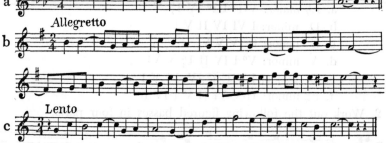

4. Harmonize the following soprano parts:

Andante

a

Allegretto

b

Lento

c

Eleven | HARMONIC RHYTHM

IT is assumed that the conceptions meter and rhythm are understood. Meter is simply measure. Meter has no rhythm. But music so often has a rhythmic pulse with which the meter coincides at important points that we think the meter is rhythmic. We then speak of strong and weak beats of the measures, forgetting that the rhythm of the music came first, and that afterwards came the effort to place the bar-line at points of rhythmic stress. Obviously, the first beat of a measure should receive rhythmic stress only when the music calls for it, and not because it happens to be the first beat.

The reaction of many influences, important among them dance music and dance forms, combined in the eighteenth and nineteenth centuries to instill the idea of regular pulse (recurring symmetrical beats) into all music. The period of harmonic practice which we are studying is at the same time the period in which there held sway the greatest "tyranny of the bar-line." Composers of earlier centuries worked with free and flexible rhythms like those of fine prose, and in the twentieth century there has been an attempt to recapture the principle of that higher organization of rhythm; but from Bach to Franck it cannot be denied that the rule is regularity of beats and of measures.

That we are still far from an appreciation of the subtleties and mastery of rhythm even under our conventionalized system, shown in the works of the best composers, is largely due to our acceptance of the doctrine of strong and weak beats as a substitute for the open-minded appraisal of the rhythmic values of each individual musical

phrase. The study of rhythm is rendered more complex by the phenome-
non of up and down beats. Either of these may be strong or weak,
which is to say that rhythmic stress may possess the feeling of up or
down. We try to place the bar-lines so that strong down-beats come
as first beats of the measures, but musical notation provides no way
of indicating when this is not so.

It is difficult to reconcile the rhythms of the following examples
with the familiar classification of beats of the measure into strong,
weak, and weaker.

EX. 241. Bach—*Sarabande from the Second English Suite*

Here, as we know by tradition to be characteristic of the sarabande,
the stress is on the second beat of the measure. The third beat is
entirely without accent, the effect of the measure being that of a
short first beat followed by a heavy second beat lasting twice as
long.

EX. 242. Mozart—*Overture to "The Magic Flute"*

Here the only accent is on the fourth quarter, the six eighth-notes
being all of equal rhythmic value. Mozart has underlined the natural
rhythm by marking the accented sixteenth-note group *forte*. To suggest that the bar-line should be located before this accent, which is
clearly a strong up-beat, would be unthinkable.

EX. 243. Brahms—*Capriccio, op. 116, no. 3*

In this example, the second beat of the first measure is at least as strongly accented as the first beat. There is no stress at all on the first beat of the second measure, the down-beat, and the ensuing three quarters serve as up-beat (anacrusis) to the third measure. Thus the second measure begins with a weak down-beat.

RHYTHMIC TEXTURE OF MUSIC

In its total effect on the listener, the rhythm of music derives from two main sources, melodic and harmonic. We omit from this discussion the percussive resource, exemplified by the bass-drum stroke, not because it has not been significantly employed, but because its habitual role has been to heighten or underline either melodic or harmonic rhythms.

Examination of the following example will show these two kinds of rhythm.

EX. 244. Beethoven—*Sonata, op. 31, no. 3*

The melodic rhythms here combined may be indicated thus:

EX. 245

The four patterns are clearly not in agreement as to accents or points of rhythmic stress.

Taking the Roman numerals of the harmonic analysis as indicating the distribution of the root changes in the phrase, we can write the pattern of the harmonic rhythm thus:

EX. 246

Admitting the inadequacy of this merely quantitative notation of rhythm, there are nevertheless two significant observations to be made:

a. The pattern of harmonic rhythm, although differing from each of the patterns of melodic rhythm, is the product of the combination of these. This is an excellent corroboration of the often-repeated statement that chords are made by moving voices. On the other hand, it is entirely feasible to reverse the process. The composer may have started with the harmonic pattern and have derived from it the melodic lines.

b. The root changes, which give the rhythmic pattern of the harmony, are not regular in time, like a regular pulse, nor are they of equal rhythmic value, quite apart from the unequal time values they possess. Both of these aspects of harmonic rhythm, frequency of change of root and the quality of that change, must receive attention in a study of harmony as used by composers.

MELODIC RHYTHM

There need not be as much diversity in patterns as found in the Beethoven example. It is true that rhythmic independence of melodic lines is the test of good counterpoint, but music is not always contrapuntal and the complexity of its texture varies between wide limits.

The rhythmic outline of all the voices may coincide, in which case the resultant harmonic rhythm will be in agreement with the melodic rhythm, although not necessarily with the meter.

EX. 247. Beethoven—*Sonata, op. 53*

harmonic rhythm:

EX. 248

EX. 249. Schumann—*Symphony no. 1*

harmonic rhythm:

EX. 250

In the above examples the top voice is heard as a melody. This is called homophonic music, as distinguished from polyphonic music, in which two or more independent melodic lines are heard in combination.

When all else is subordinated to one melodic line we have melody and accompaniment. The accompaniment is frequently lacking in rhythmic interest, to avoid lessening the prominence of the melody. The following is an example of flexibility in melodic rhythm combined with regularity in the root changes of the harmonic rhythm.

EX. 251. Chopin—*Nocturne, op. 48, no. 1*

harmonic rhythm:

EX. 252

In the latter part of the nineteenth century some composers became interested in complicated part-writing of a chromatic nature, and, in their efforts to conceal the underlying harmony and increase the contrapuntal interest, obscured and even obliterated the feeling of harmonic progression. Whether deliberate or inadvertent, this amounted to an impoverishment of the rhythmic life of the music.

For vitality of contrapuntal texture over a clear harmonic rhythmic background, the works of J. S. Bach remain the models of perfection throughout the period.

EX. 253. Bach—*Well-tempered Clavier, I, Fugue no. 1*

harmonic rhythm:
EX. 254

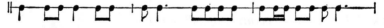

Frequency of root change and rhythmic quality of the changes are, then, the two main features of harmonic rhythm. When the harmony changes with much frequency the effect is apt to be one of restlessness.

EX. 255. Beethoven—*Thirty-three Variations, op. 120*

harmonic rhythm:

EX. 256

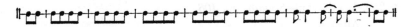

Widely spaced changes of harmony give the impression of breadth and relaxation.

EX. 257. Mozart—*Symphony, K. no. 550*

harmonic rhythm:

EX. 258

STATIC HARMONY

There are instances of complete absence of harmonic rhythm throughout whole sections of a composition. One of the most famous examples of this effect of static harmony is the prelude to Wagner's music drama *Das Rheingold,* where the chord of E-flat major serves as the unchanging background of the entire prelude, one hundred and thirty-six measures in moderate tempo.

Static harmony, or absence of harmonic rhythm, is more often felt as a defect in music by composers of inferior gifts. Like all other technical resources, it is bound to be ineffective when the result of indifference or unawareness on the part of the composer. On the other hand, it is successful when appropriately used. Often it arises from the elaboration of a single chord, as in the following example.

EX. 259. Beethoven—*Sonata, op. 106*

The rhythmic quality of the harmonic change is influenced by a number of factors, often of no little subtlety and open to differences of opinion as to their values, but it is of prime importance to the student if he aspires to an insight into the function of harmony as a musical means.

TIME VALUES

First among these factors is the agogic element, the effect of time. Long and short values, it is generally agreed, are synonymous with heavy and light, strong and weak, rhythmic quantities. Down and up, in terms of beats, should not be included in this parallel.

EX. 260

strong   weak   strong   weak

The application of the principle of long and short values to chords on the same root imparts a rhythm, but this should not be thought of as harmonic rhythm, which has to do with harmonic changes, that is, changes of root.

EX. 261. Beethoven—*Symphony no. 7*

STRONG AND WEAK PROGRESSIONS

From a purely harmonic standpoint, the basic factor in rhythm is the inherent rhythmic value of each harmonic progression. These values seldom exist in music without the influence of other factors but they may be brought out by playing the progressions in their simplest forms.

As remarked in the case of the cadential six-four chord, a strong progression is one which gives the impression of weak (light) proceeding to strong (heavy). In general, the progressions with root moving by fourth, fifth, or second are strong progressions.

EX. 262

II V   V I   I V   IV I   V VI   V IV

A progression with root moving up a third is a weak progression, giving a rhythmic impression of strong to weak.

EX. 263

VI I III V

The progressions with root moving down a third are not definitely either weak or strong.

EX. 264

I VI IV II

These qualifications as weak or strong are incomplete as descriptions of the rhythmic value of any progression unless we observe also its feeling of up or down. The fact is that any progression is capable of being sensed as down-up or up-down (see Ex. 260).

When more than two chords are involved, the possibilities in shades of rhythmic meaning are multiplied. The following example shows a grouping of strong progressions, with bar-lines suggesting some rhythmic interpretations of up and down to which the progressions are susceptible. Let us repeat that the bar-line is but an indicator of the interpretation and not a cause of it.

EX. 265

With the limited materials now at his command the student will not be expected to apply advanced principles of harmonic rhythm. It is advisable at this point, however, to mention some other rhythmic influences which will surely be present in almost any music that is examined.

DISSONANCE

Dissonance is contrapuntal in principle, and it is an important element in motion. The dissonant chord and its resolution may compose either an up-down or a down-up progression. The harmonic rhythm is concerned with root movement and is either confirmed or contradicted by the polyphonic superstructure.

EX. 266

V_7 I V_7 I

DYNAMIC INDICATIONS

Directions for nuances of loud and soft, *crescendi* and *diminuendi,* accents, *sforzandi,* and the like, are of course not elements of harmonic rhythm. Their use is ordinarily to confirm and accentuate the natural rhythmic feeling already present in the music, although sometimes for a particular expressive purpose the composer may employ them in a contrary sense.

EX. 267. Beethoven—*Sonata, op. 31, no. 3*

harmonic rhythm:

EX. 268

In the above example the second chord, although a dominant seventh chord, is in a position and inversion which would allow of its complete absorption into the tonic chord, the soprano and bass being passing tones and the alto an auxiliary. The accent indicated by Beethoven would probably never have occurred to the player if no dynamic signs had been given.

PASSING CHORDS

The question raised by the Beethoven example, of whether a vertical combination of tones is an independent chord, or just some melodic tones which happen to harmonize at the moment, depends upon various considerations and is often open to differing interpretations. It will have to be decided mainly on rhythmic grounds, but one should take into consideration the general pace and musical intent of the piece.

In this example the speed of the music justifies a broader view of the harmony, so that the harmonic meter of one chord per measure seems reasonable.

EX. 269. Scarlatti—*Sonata*

harmonic rhythm:

EX. 270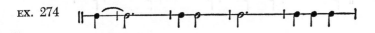

On the other hand, in a slow tempo the passing chords are dwelt upon long enough to give them harmonic significance.

EX. 271. Haydn—*Sonata*

harmonic rhythm:

EX. 272

PEDALS

The pedal effect, where a tone, usually the bass, is held through harmonies which are foreign to it, is rhythmically static, since it tends to deprive the harmonic progressions above of their basses and to cause them to be heard as melodic tones over a single root. However, the changes of harmony in the upper voices may succeed in offsetting the static feeling of the pedal by asserting their independent harmonic rhythm.

EX. 273. Chopin—*Mazurka, op. 6, no. 4*

harmonic rhythm of upper parts:

EX. 274

SYNCOPATION

Syncopation implies a well-established rhythmic pulse, the effect being based on a dislocation of that pulse by giving a strong accent where one is not expected, and suppressing the normal accent of the pulse.

There are four ways in which syncopation may be employed.

1. The principal melodic line may be syncopated against the harmonic rhythm, or pulse.

EX. 275. Schubert—*String Quartet, op. 29*

harmonic rhythm:

EX. 276

2. The pulse may not be actually heard but may exist by analogy with the preceding measures.

EX. 277. Beethoven—*Sonata, op. 101*

harmonic rhythm:

EX. 278

3. Both melodic and harmonic rhythms may be syncopated against a pulse previously established but not heard at the moment.

EX. 279. Brahms—*Intermezzo, op. 118, no. 2*

A:I   VI   IV   II   I

harmonic rhythm:

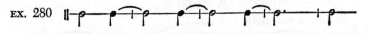

EX. 280

4. The harmonic rhythm may be syncopated, while the rhythm of the melody continues to agree with the established pulse.

EX. 281. Chopin—*Prelude, op. 28, no. 4*

E: IV   II   V

harmonic rhythm:

EX. 282

EX. 283. Beethoven—*Symphony no. 9*

B♭:V⁷ I—VI IV ———— V⁶₅ofV —— I⁶₄ —— V⁷ ———— VofVI

harmonic rhythm:

EX. 284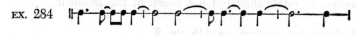

THE ANACRUSIS

The common term for anacrusis is up-beat, as opposed to thesis, meaning down-beat. Up and down are good descriptions of the rhythmic effects produced by anacrusis and thesis, probably because we instinctively think of a conductor's stick, or a violinist's bow. Rhythmically, however, these terms should not be taken to mean weak and strong, respectively. The up-beat may be strong, introducing a weak down-beat.

EX. 285. Brahms—*Intermezzo, op. 76, no. 6*

harmonic rhythm:

EX. 286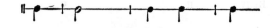

Or it may be weak rhythmically, the stress coming on the down-beat.

EX. 287. Schumann—*Album for the Young, no. 30*

harmonic rhythm:

EX. 288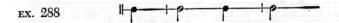

EXERCISES

1. Write phrases in four parts, having the following patterns of harmonic rhythm and employing the harmonies suggested by the given numerals:

a
C minor: I V   VI   IV II   I V I   V

b
G major: IV   II V   III VI III   VI I IV   V   I

c
C major: V I V I   IV I III   VI   VI II   I⁶₄ II V   I

2. Write phrases in four parts, having the following patterns of harmonic rhythm and employing optional harmonies:

3. Work out the following figured basses in four parts:

4. Harmonize the following unfigured basses:

5. Harmonize the following soprano parts:

Twelve | MODULATION

COMPOSERS appear to have been in consistent agreement that to remain in one key throughout a piece of any length is aesthetically undesirable. The process of modulation, meaning change of key, is one of the most important resources of variety in music.

A change of key means a change of tonal center, the adoption of a different tone to which all the other tones are to be related.

Any chord, or any group of tones, can be interpreted in any key. This is but another way of saying that a relationship can be found between any given chord and any one of the twelve tones chosen as a tonal center, or key-note. The ambiguity of the single chord was pointed out in the discussion of tonality, and it is just this ambiguity which is the basis of the technique of modulation.

Taking the triad of C major, the following interpretations can be given it without using more advanced chords than those which have already been used by the student:

EX. 289

C I, F V, G IV, A III, E VI, and D VII (descending minor).

The relationships to the other six tones are given here for completeness, but require a knowledge of chromatic alterations: C-sharp: V of III; E-flat: V of II; E: V of the Neapolitan sixth; A-flat: V of VI; B-flat: V of V; B:II Neapolitan sixth.

The above are not the only relationships existing in each case, but are offered as examples to show the principle.

There are three stages in the mental process of effecting a modulation within a phrase. First, a tonality has to be made clear to the hearer. Second, the composer at some point changes his tonal center. Third, the hearer is made aware of the change, and the new tonal center is made clear to him.

THE INITIAL KEY

In the first stage, the establishment of the first key, the principles described in the chapter on tonality should be observed. It is not essential that the tonic chord should appear, but the dominant must be made to sound as such. Indecision due to overuse of modal degrees and their harmonies may result in the whole phrase being heard as in the second key, especially if the second key is strongly established.

When the phrase containing the modulation is not the first phrase of the piece there is less responsibility to establish the first key, provided that it is the key of the preceding cadence.

THE PIVOT CHORD

The second stage of the modulation involves the choice of a chord which will be conveniently susceptible to the change of tonal viewpoint. In other words, it will be a chord common to both keys, which we will call the pivot chord, and to which we will give a double analysis.

For example, the C major triad could be employed as a pivot chord in a modulation from C to G, indicated thus:

EX. 290

$$\begin{cases} C: & I \\ G: & IV \end{cases}$$

The pivot chord selected is preferably not the V of the second key. In the second stage we are still at the point where only the composer is aware that a modulation is to take place. The sounding of the dominant chord of the new key belongs to a later stage, when the hearer is made to realize that a new tonal center is being felt. To put it a little more technically, the pivot chord should be placed in advance of the appearance of the dominant chord of the new key.

The following scheme represents a modulation effected by means of the pivot chord shown above:

EX. 291   C: IV II V {C: I
                        {G: IV II V I

THE NEW KEY

Establishment of the new key is accomplished by means of the cadence which ends the phrase, although there may occur strong progressions in the key before the cadence. The cadence may be any one of the types studied in Chapter Ten.

EXAMPLES OF MODULATING PHRASES

EX. 292. Bach—*Chorale: Gott sei uns gnädig*

Pattern:

EX. 293

This phrase modulates down a minor third (or up a major sixth), a change from a major key to its relative minor. After the strong tonic and dominant chords of A major, the key previously established, the supertonic triad is used as a pivot chord and looked upon as the subdominant of F-sharp minor. As such it introduces the cadential six-four chord in the fourth measure. The authentic cadence in F-sharp is made more conclusive by the plagal cadence acting as an extension of the final tonic. The major third in the tonic chord is known as the Picardy third (see Ex. 81 in Chapter Four).

EX. 294. Mozart—*Fantasia, K. 397*

Pattern:

EX. 295

This is a modulation up a perfect fifth, or from a given key to the key of its dominant. The key of D is unmistakably established by the progression I–IV–V–I. I of D is identical with IV of A, so it is taken as the pivot chord, and it introduces the V of the new key, making the strong tonal progression IV–V in A. The phrase ends with the authentic cadence strengthened by the II preceding the V–I.

EX. 296. Bach—*French Suite no. 3, Menuet*

Pattern:

EX. 297

B: I V I V I V I V I {B:IV
                        {D:II V I V I

Here the modulation is up a minor third, from a minor key to its relative major. The I–V progression in itself would not be sufficient to establish B as the tonic, if it were not for the numerous repetitions and the fact that B was the tonic of the preceding phrase. The pivot chord here is IV, which is translated into II of D, and proceeds to V.

EX. 298. Beethoven—*String Quartet, op. 18, no. 3*

Allegro

D: I I II V² I V I I

{D: VI V I V I
{F♯ IV

Pattern:

EX. 299

D:I I II V I V I I {D: VI
                          {F♯IV V I V I

A modulation up a major third. The progression II–V–I confirms the key of D. The pivot chord is VI of the major mode and is taken to be the equivalent of IV in F-sharp, minor mode. Then follows the strong progression IV–V–I in the new key.

EX. 300. Bach—*Chorale: Christus ist erstanden*

F: I   VI   I II V I {F:V G:IV VII⁶(V) I   II V   VI

Pattern:

EX. 301

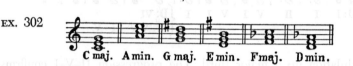

C I   VI   I II V I   V {F:III I   II V   VI
                              G: II

In this excerpt modulating down a major second, the first phrase
is shown with its strong cadence in F major. Therefore the first chord
of measure three may be taken as V, and at the same time as subdominant of G minor, with a major third, sixth degree of the ascending
minor scale. The new key is here affirmed by a deceptive cadence.

RELATED KEYS

All keys are related. It is only a question of the degree of relationship. The common expression "related keys" means always those most
closely related.

The relationship of keys has two aspects of definition. The first
conception is based on the number of tones in common between two
keys. Thus it is plain that the keys C major and G major are very
closely related since they differ in scale only as to F and F-sharp. By
this definition the keys of nearest relationship to a given key are
those having one sharp (or flat) more or less in the signature.

Major Mode

EX. 302

C maj. A min. G maj. E min. F maj. D min.

It will be noted that the key-notes in the above example comprise
the steps of the scale of C major, with the exception of VII, and that

the modes of the keys, as shown by their tonic chords, are in agreement with the triads on the scale degrees of C major. The minor key having the same signature as a major key is called its relative minor. The "family" of keys in the above illustration can be described in this way: tonic (major); dominant; subdominant; and the relative minors of all three.

Minor Mode

EX. 303

A min. C maj. E min. G maj. D min. F maj.

The keys having one sharp (or flat) more or less than a minor key show two important differences. The second degree is missing. It will be remembered that II in the minor mode is a diminished triad and could not serve as a tonic chord. The seventh degree, however, is present, not in its form as leading-tone triad but as a major triad on the seventh degree found in the descending melodic scale. Its relationship is that of relative major of the dominant. This "family" of keys may be described thus: tonic (minor); dominant; subdominant; and the relative majors of all three.

INTERCHANGE OF MODES

During the nineteenth century, as more interest in harmonic color developed, the latent potentialities of another aspect of key-relationship were exploited. This is the closeness of the major mode to the minor mode having the same tonic. Under the principles just outlined, the keys C major and C minor are rather distantly related since there is a difference of three flats in the signature. We have seen, however, that these two keys are practically identical, having as they do the same tonal degrees and really differing only in the third degree. Practice in the nineteenth century, and much individual practice in the eighteenth, tends to regard the two modes as simply two aspects of one tonality, so that the "family" of keys is greatly enlarged.

Rather than compile a list of related keys under this broader principle it is more practical to consider each pair of keys individually. The method of appraising the relationship of a second key to a main tonality is the same as that of relating a chord to a given tonality. The new tonic note is interpreted as in the fundamental key, together with its particular form as a chord.

These are a few examples:

D major is related to C minor as dominant of the dominant.

A-flat major is related to C major as minor sixth degree.

G minor is related to C major as dominant minor, or as subdominant of the second degree, or as supertonic of the subdominant, etc.

In this way tonalities themselves can be said to possess tonal functions in relation to one another, which partly explains the care which composers have customarily bestowed upon the key-scheme of a composition. Modulation is an element of variety but also of unity when the balance of the keys in support of a main tonality is used to advantage. The key-scheme, or pattern of keys, is therefore one of the most significant ingredients of form.

EXPLORATION OF MEANS

The steps given show how the composer modulates by adopting a new tonal center for a given chord. The problem is slightly different when two tonalities are given and the pivot chord is to be found. Here, as in all branches of theoretical study, it is urged that no steps be omitted. They should rather be dwelt upon for what can be learned from them. It is natural to take advantage of the first good pivot chord that comes to mind, and it may happen that none better could be found. But the student should be advised and even required at least a few times to find all the possible pivot chords between two given keys, and then to select the one he considers the most effective to use.

Since we are still limiting ourselves to triads, while establishing fundamental principles, the exhaustive list of pivot chords between two keys will not be very large. The process of discovering these involves the attempted interpretation of all the chords of the first key, in terms of the second key.

Assuming the two keys to be C and B-flat, we first write all the forms of the triads we know in C and note those for which we find an explanation in the key of B-flat.

EX. 304

Looking at these possibilities, we can say at once that the B-flat V is not very good, since it is preferable to locate the pivot chord in advance of the dominant of the new key. The B-flat II would be excellent for the second key, but, as it is the minor form of I in C, it would be convenient only if we wished to leave the impression of the minor mode in the first key. The B-flat I is not without objection— the note B-flat would have to appear in C as part of the descending melodic minor scale, and to make that clear it would have to proceed next to A-flat, a note we do not particularly welcome in B-flat. These considerations leave the two remaining possibilities B-flat III and IV. Since IV contains the troublesome note B-flat, that leaves B-flat III, or in other words II of C, as best choice for the pivot chord.

ABRUPT MODULATIONS

Modulation means change of key. Hence there cannot be a "change of key without modulation." Some modulations sound sudden and unexpected, and sometimes one feels that the composer did not intend an overlapping transition between the two keys. But there can be no modulation in which the last chord of the first key cannot be analyzed in terms of the second key, as a pivot chord. By this process the harmonic progression at the point of modulation is accurately described, and the degree of suddenness brought to light.

The following example is not one of an abrupt modulation, but the turn in the cadential measure from B major to D major is certainly unexpected, and it loses none of its charm with repeated hearings. Following the excerpt here given, the orchestra continues on the dominant harmony of D major.

EX. 305. Beethoven—*Symphony no. 9*

ENHARMONIC MODULATIONS

In modulations between flat keys and sharp keys the pivot chord
will often require enharmonic reading in one of the keys. The example below shows a modulation from D-flat major (five flats) to A major
(three sharps). The pivot chord is notated as an F-sharp minor triad,
VI of A, whereas in the first key it would be a G-flat minor triad,
IV (minor) of D-flat. The notes would be G-flat, B-double-flat, D-flat.

EX. 306. Schubert—*Sonata no. 10*

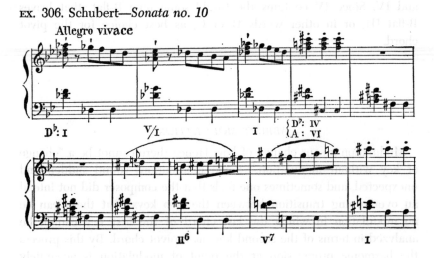

EXERCISES

1. Interpret the triad at top of page 149 in as many keys as possible, using Roman numerals.

2. Label the triad below as a pivot chord in as many modulations as possible.

3. Work out the following figured basses:

4. Write out in Roman numerals the scheme of a phrase modulating in each of the following ways (four separate phrases in all), using only triads:

    a. The pivot chord is II of the second key.

    b. The pivot chord is V of the first key.

    c. The modulation is to a key a perfect fourth above the original key.

    d. The modulation is to a key a minor third above the original key.

5. a. Analyze the phrase by Schumann, given below.

    b. Write out the pattern of the harmonic rhythm of the phrase.

    c. Construct the four-part harmonic scheme.

    d. Using this harmonic pattern, construct a new phrase different from the original.

Schumann—*Album for the Young, op. 68, no. 17*

6. Show by Roman numerals the relationship of all the chords in A major to the tonality of C-sharp minor.

7. Write in four parts the following phrases:

a C min. $\frac{2}{2}$ VI ⫶ IV II ⫶ V ⫶ { I ⫶ ⫶ ⫶ ⫶ ‖
                                      { III ⫶ IV II ⫶ V ⫶ I

b E maj. $\frac{3}{4}$ I V I ⫶ IV II ⫶ { V ⫶ ⫶ ⫶ ‖
                                        { IV I IV ⫶ V ⫶ I

c B♭maj. $\frac{4}{4}$ V VI II ⫶ V I ⫶ { VI ⫶ ⫶ ‖
                                          { II VI IV ⫶ V ⫶ I

Thirteen | THE DOMINANT SEVENTH CHORD

ALTHOUGH seventh chords may be built by superposing an interval of a third upon a triad, it must not be concluded that these chords originated by that process. It should be repeated that chords are made by moving voices. The seventh, the factor which gives its name to the seventh chord, first appeared as a melodic, nonharmonic tone. In the case of the seventh chord on the dominant, the seventh is often seen in this purely melodic capacity.

EX. 307

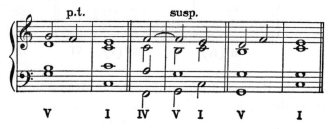

EX. 308. Handel—*Suite no. 8, Courante*

The next evolutionary step was naturally the inclusion into the harmonic vocabulary of the vertical cross-section G–B–D–F as a chord, which we call V_7. Its complete figuring is $V\,{}_{3}^{7}{}_{5}$ if we wish to show all the factors by numerals.

The adoption of V_7 as an independent chord brings to the vocabulary the first unequivocal harmonic dissonance. With three exceptions all dissonances we have been using are nonharmonic, contrapuntal dissonances, tones foreign to the chords with which they are sounded. The seventh of V_7 adds a dissonant element to the chord itself, so it is a harmonic dissonance.

The three exceptions are the dissonant diminished triads VII and II (in minor) and the augmented triad III (in minor). The leading-tone triad may be disposed of at once by declaring it to be an incomplete dominant seventh. It certainly sounds and acts as a dominant.

It has been argued that II of the minor mode is used chiefly in first inversion, with the second degree standing as a nonharmonic tone for the tonic note in a chord of the subdominant. Likewise the third degree in III of the minor mode, also in first inversion, is described as an appoggiatura in a dominant chord.

EX. 309

$\text{II}^6(\text{IV})$ V III^6 (V)   VI

Whatever the theoretical explanation, we are bound to report the use of these dissonant triads by composers, even in root position, where the above reasoning is more difficult of application.

There are present in the dominant seventh chord two dissonant intervals: the diminished fifth between third and seventh, and the minor seventh between root and seventh. It has been common practice to resolve these dissonances.

The principle of resolution has two aspects, harmonic and melodic.

Harmonically, the dissonant intervals are followed in resolution by consonant intervals.

Melodically, that is to say contrapuntally, the tendency tones set up by the dissonant intervals move in the direction of their tendencies to a point where they are no longer dissonant and no longer have the tendency to move.

The tendency of the diminished fifth is to contract to a third, major or minor, both voices moving inward by step. If the leading-tone, the lower of the two voices, alone moved, the following interval would still be dissonant, the perfect fourth.

In the case of the seventh, it would be possible for the upper voice alone to move, downward by step according to its tendency. This would leave the imperfect consonance, major or minor sixth. When the lower note, the dominant, moves up to the tonic a more satisfactory interval is reached, the third.

EX. 310

5 4   5 3   7 6   7 3

Inversion of these two dissonant intervals gives an augmented fourth and a major second, or ninth if the voices are further apart. The tendencies of the tones remain the same, so that the augmented fourth will expand to a sixth and the major second will become a third.

EX. 311

4 6   2 3

Let us consider the contrapuntal consequences of disregarding the tendency of the seventh to descend. The following relative melodic movements would result:

EX. 312

5 5   7 5   2 1   9 8

The two fifths should not be referred to as parallel fifths. Strictly speaking, the voices are not parallel, one fifth being smaller than the other. The characteristics to be noted in this progression are, first, the improper resolution of the tendency of the two voices in the dissonant interval, and, second, the prominence of the perfect fifth approached by similar motion. The same comment applies to the resolution of the seventh by similar motion to the fifth. It is a general rule that these relative melodic progressions are avoided.

The resolution of the second into the unison is used only when it is a minor second, and the upper voice is a nonharmonic anticipation.

EX. 313

G: V   I

EX. 314. Bach—Chorale: *Alle Menschen müssen sterben*

D: I   IV   V   VI⁷ V⁴₃of V V   IVI   II   I⁶   II⁶₅   V   I

An interval of a ninth is followed by an octave only when it is the upper voice that moves.

EX. 315

9   8

REGULAR RESOLUTION

All dissonant chords have what is called a regular resolution. Harmonically, the term means the chord to which the dissonant chord usually progresses. It is best expressed in terms of root progression.

The regular resolution of V_7 to I is probably the most fundamental harmonic progression in music. It is without doubt the commonest, and it seems to be felt instinctively as a natural musical word even by an unmusical person.

The presence of the fourth degree, subdominant, supplies the only important tonal factor that was missing in V–I; hence this is the perfect progression for the definition of tonality.

In the resolution, the seventh descends one degree. The third ascends to the tonic and the fifth of the chord, having no tendency, descends to the tonic rather than double the modal third degree. This results in an incomplete chord of resolution. It is to be remarked, however, that the tonal balance of three roots and one third is always preferred to that of two roots and two thirds, quite apart from the precedence of contrapuntal movement that caused the doubling. The principle of doubling tonal degrees in preference to modal degrees is thus corroborated.

EX. 316

EX. 317. Mozart—*Symphony, K. 551*

The second degree, fifth of the chord, is not essential to the satisfactory sonority of the dominant seventh chord, and is frequently omitted. The consequent doubling of the root gives a convenient common tone between the two chords, and the repetition of this common tone supplies the missing fifth to the tonic chord.

EX. 318

Omission of the third is less often practiced, but there are occasions when the melodic outline of the voices brings about such a disposition. The chord is clearly recognizable as a dominant seventh and is a little less thick in sonority.

If it is particularly desired that the tonic chord contain the fifth, as for instance in the final chord of a movement, the leading-tone is made to descend to the dominant—only, however, when it is in the alto or the tenor voice. Here the harmonic aspect assumes more importance to the composer than the melodic aspect (see EX. 308).

EX. 319

G: V⁷   I   E♭: V⁷   I

When the dominant seventh chord resolves to a tonic chord in first inversion, the bass may be said to have taken over the resolution of the seventh. The seventh may not resolve as usual because of the resultant direct octave on the third degree. It therefore moves upward, making the direct fifth and also the incorrect resolution of the diminished fifth, unless this interval happens to be in its inversion as an augmented fourth.

EX. 320

F: V⁷   I⁶   V⁷   I⁶

This resolution, which is not at all uncommon, is classified as a variant of the regular resolution, but it contains the above-described irregularities of contrapuntal movement.

THE FIRST INVERSION

The first inversion of the dominant seventh chord is commonly called the "dominant six-five," its complete figuring being V^6_5. The 3 is often omitted as understood.

Factors are rarely omitted from inversions of seventh chords. The root, since it is in an inside voice, will be repeated in the next chord so that the tonic chord of resolution will be complete. All other circumstances aside, the dominant six-five-three is most effective when the original seventh of the chord is in the soprano voice.

EX. 321

EX. 322. Haydn—*Symphony no. 6, "Surprise"*

It will be noticed that the tendency tones move just as they did in the root position resolution.

This inversion is useful in constructing a melodic bass and also as a relief to the weight of the root position progression.

THE SECOND INVERSION

The inversion with the fifth in the bass is called the "four-three" chord. The complete figuring shows the intervals six, four, and three: V_{4}^{6}.

It is generally considered weaker rhythmically than the other inversions, and it is very often used as a passing chord between I and I_6.

In this case, the bass is normally treated as a passing tone between the tonic and the third degree, moving either up or down. The other voices follow their tendencies as before, the exception being that when the bass moves up to I_6 the seventh resolves upward in the same way and with the same contrapuntal results as in the progression V_7–I_6.

EX. 323

EX. 324. Beethoven—*String Quartet, op. 130*

EX. 325. Bach—*St. Matthew Passion*

The following example shows the V^4_3 chord as what might be called an auxiliary chord, the bass being melodically an auxiliary tone.

EX. 326. Haydn—*String Quartet, op. 76, no. 4*

In the example below, by Schubert, this inversion of the dominant seventh is used for its characteristic sound, as an important chord in the phrase.

EX. 327. Schubert—*String Quartet, op. 29*

THE THIRD INVERSION

The third inversion, with the seventh in the bass, is a strong chord. The bass is here dissonant with two of the upper voices and is thereby given a strong tendency to move. A significant comparison can be drawn between the dissonant quality of this bass with that of the bass of the second inversion. In the second inversion the bass is the lower note of the dissonant perfect fourth, in which the top note possesses the tendency to descend. The bass is therefore free to move up or down. In the third inversion the bass is the lower note of two dissonant intervals, the augmented fourth and the major second, and in each case has the obligation to move downward one degree. Hence this is a strong chord with an unusually strong tendency in a certain direction.

The other voices move as before, except that a favorite soprano part for this progression is one that moves from supertonic up a fourth to dominant, doubling the fifth in I_6.

The full figuring of the chord is V^6_4, usually abbreviated to V_2, or V^4_2.

EX. 328

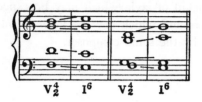

EX. 329. Beethoven—*Sonata, op. 13*

A♭: I   V² 　 I⁶ 　 V⁶₅ 　 I V⁶ VI VofV V

The following apparent resolutions are but the effect of auxiliary tones over a static harmony.

EX. 330. Mendelssohn—*Italian Symphony*

E: V² 　 (I⁶) 　 V² 　 (I⁶) 　 V²

PREPARATION OF DISSONANCES

A great deal has been said and written about the preparation of dissonances. Theorists are agreed that dissonances are to be resolved, but opinions vary on the question of preparation.

Let us say at once that the composers themselves show considerable variety in their attitude toward the preparation of dissonance. The period of harmonic common practice is decidedly not a period of common practice in counterpoint. The preparation or nonpreparation of dissonance is a detail of style which may be expected to vary with different composers and which may be inconsistent in two works of different purpose by the same composer.

EX. 331. Bach—*Well-tempered Clavier, I, Prelude no. 24*

dissonances unprepared
B: V   I⁶   V⁶ {B: V⁶ of IV   V⁶   VI
                       {F♯: IV

EX. 332. Bach—*Well-tempered Clavier, I, Fugue no. 24*

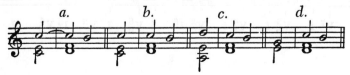

dissonances prepared
B: I   V   II   V   I   VI²   II   V⁷

A dissonance is perfectly prepared when it enters as a suspension
(a).

Next to that it may enter as a repeated tone (b).

It is prepared, although less perfectly, if it enters by step (c).

It is not prepared if it enters by skip (d).

EX. 333

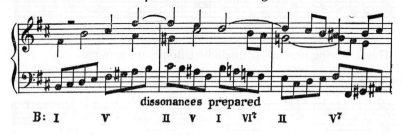

Distinction must be made between harmonic and nonharmonic
dissonances. The nonharmonic tones, which are usually dissonant,
have their own characteristics of preparation and resolution. It is
with the harmonic dissonances, like the seventh in the dominant
seventh chord, that the question of preparation arises. The student
is advised to apply all the degrees of preparation in the written exercises. It will be especially instructive to make alternative versions
of the progressions involving harmonic dissonance, in order to test
the effect of preparation and nonpreparation on the general style.

THE MELODIC TRITONE

A melodic fragment that is included in the limits of an augmented fourth, from subdominant to seventh degree, is almost invariably resolved in the melodic line, either by the leading-tone continuing to the tonic, or, in descending, by the fourth degree continuing to the third.

EX. 334

The following unresolved melodic tritones are avoided:

EX. 335

Formulae, to be played in all keys:

EXERCISES

1. Work out in four parts the following figured basses:

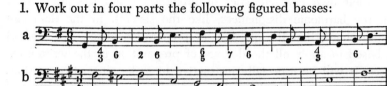

2. Construct a musical sentence of two phrases according to the following specifications:

a. The first phrase begins in G major and ends with an authentic cadence in E minor.

b. The second phrase returns to G major by means of a pivot chord which is the supertonic triad in G.

c. One example of each of the three inversions of the dominant seventh chord is introduced appropriately.

3. Construct a musical sentence of two phrases according to the following specifications:

a. The first phrase ends with a deceptive cadence, without modulation.

b. The first phrase shows the resolution of V_7 to I_6.

c. The second phrase shows two uses of the V_2 chord—with the seventh prepared and with the seventh unprepared.

4. Harmonize the following basses, introducing dominant seventh chords and inversions:

Moderato

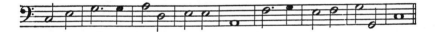

Allegretto

5. Harmonize the following soprano parts:

a

Andantino

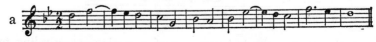

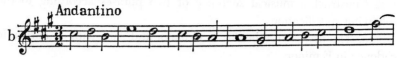

Moderato

c

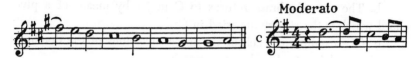

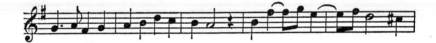

Fourteen | SECONDARY DOMINANTS

ALMOST any page of music chosen at random will show the presence of numerous accidentals, sharps, flats, and natural signs, which indicate alterations of the tones other than the qualifications announced by the key signature. We know that these chromatic signs do not necessarily signify that a modulation has taken place. Some of them are accounted for as the required notation of the leading-tone in the minor mode. Others are seen to be alterations of nonharmonic tones, like the auxiliary acting as temporary leading-tone beneath the principal note.

Perhaps the largest source of these accidental signs lies in the tendency of composers to prefer the sound of dominant harmony to that of nondominant function, a tendency which prevailed throughout the period on which we base our harmonic theory. The procedure gave harmonic color by the addition of new notes and increased the sense of direction and movement in the harmony. In its extreme form it produced a harmonic scheme in which each chord became the dominant of the next.

EX. 336. Mozart—*Sonata, K. 283*

From observation of this practice of composers the following rule may be stated: Any degree of the scale may be preceded by its own dominant harmony without weakening the fundamental tonality.

These temporary dominant chords have been referred to by theorists as attendant chords, parenthesis chords, borrowed chords, etc. We shall call them secondary dominants, in the belief that the term is slightly more descriptive of their function.

Far from weakening the tonality, the secondary dominants can be a distinct aid in strengthening it. If we imagine a tonal center, supported on either hand by subdominant and dominant, it is easy to see that if these two important tonal degrees are in turn supported by their respective dominants the whole tonal edifice is made stronger thereby. This is essentially the scheme used by Beethoven in the opening measures of his first symphony. The actual tonic chord is delayed in its arrival, but it is made the more inevitable by the strong supports established beforehand.

EX. 337. Beethoven—*Symphony no. 1*

The secondary dominants have not only a functional value but are an important source of harmonic color as well. Composers of the eighteenth and nineteenth centuries were interested in the expressive advantages of new notes which could logically be included in the tonality. The harmonic vocabulary was greatly enriched through the introduction of these chords.

All the forms applicable to the regular dominant of the key are employed as secondary dominants. That means, at the present stage, major triads, dominant seventh chords, and the dominant seventh without root (leading-tone triad), with all inversions. For example, the chord VofV in the key of C may have these forms:

EX. 338

C: VofV

RESOLUTION

The principles of resolution in the dominant-to-tonic progression are equally valid in the treatment of secondary dominants. The secondary dominant and its tonic are considered a tonal unit of two chords for all purposes of voice leading. Thus, in the example above, the F-sharp is for the moment not the subdominant of C but the leading-tone of G, and so it is not doubled. The D is temporarily the tonal degree in the chord.

An important principle of chromatic alteration will be seen active in the treatment of secondary dominants. That is, a note chromatically raised is given thereby a tendency to proceed upward, and, conversely, a note chromatically lowered is given a tendency to proceed downward.

EX. 339

METHOD OF INTRODUCTION

The smoothest and most natural way that a secondary dominant may be introduced is from a chord which could be interpreted in the key of which the secondary dominant is the actual dominant. In this case the group of three chords (the secondary dominant as the second chord of the group) could be regarded as in the temporary tonality, but the first and third chords would still be equally strong members of the true tonality.

EX. 340

C: VI   V of V   V
G: II   V   I

Such a duality of tonal meaning facilitates the chord connection and guarantees the logical sound of the harmonic progression.

Often, however, the preceding chord is incapable of natural analysis in the temporary key. This will ordinarily mean that a chromatic relationship exists between the two chords. A tone of one will appear in chromatically altered form in the other.

CROSS-RELATION

When this chromatic relationship is found between two different voices the effect is called "cross-relation," or "false-relation."

EX. 341

cross relation

It will be recalled that this term is likewise applied to other relationships, such as the tritone, occurring between two voices instead of in one voice melodically. The expression "false-relation" is unfortunate in that it implies a defect, whereas "cross-relation" points out that the relationship exists "across" the voices. Cross-relation is found in the works of all composers of the harmonic period, but never indiscriminately used.

The various accepted uses of cross-relation will be discussed in connection with the relevant material. Here it will suffice to mention the most common. That is when the two tones involved are treated as scale degrees of the melodic and harmonic minor. In the examples above, the cross-relation would be acceptable if the key were G minor, with F-natural as descending seventh degree. A passing tone E-flat would be either written or understood between F and D. The F-sharp is, of course, the ascending leading-tone.

In C major, however, no such logic exists and this cross-relation is generally avoided. The chords would be arranged in a manner to allow the chromatic progression to take place in a single voice.

EX. 342

C: IV VofV V

The student is advised to connect such chords at first without cross-relation, but to experiment with the sound of other arrangements and to observe instances of cross-relation encountered in the works of composers.

VofII

The dominant of the second degree has for its root the sixth degree of the major scale. It is not used if the minor mode is prevalent, since in that mode the supertonic is a diminished triad and hence does not act as a tonic, even temporarily. The tonic of the key is chromatically raised to make it the leading-tone of II.

The following example shows VofII as a triad both in root position and as a passing six-four chord.

EX. 343. Schumann—*Novelette, op. 21*

F: VofII II^6 V$^6_4$ofII II V I

As a dominant six-five-three chord:

EX. 344. Liszt—*"Faust" Symphony*

A♭: V$^4_3$ VI$^6_5$ V^6 V$^6_5$ofII II I^6 V$^6_4$

V of III

As there are two third degrees, major and minor, so there will be two dominants available, a semitone apart in pitch. Needless to say, the dominant of the third degree of the minor mode does not progress to the third degree of the major mode, and vice versa.

In the major mode two alterations are necessary. The second degree is raised to become leading-tone of the third, and the fourth degree is raised to form a perfect fifth with the seventh degree root.

EX. 345. Schubert—*Symphony no. 8*

Note that the chromatically raised second and fourth degrees resolve upward, also that the chord and its resolution may be considered as the dominant-to-tonic progression in the key of G-sharp minor.

In the following instance, the chord VofIII is given the rhythmic prominence of the final chord in a cadence, as though there were a half-cadence in C-sharp. The entire chorale is, however, clearly in A, so that a change of key so soon seems hardly logical.

EX. 346. Bach—Chorale: *Es ist genug*

If the minor third degree is employed, its dominant will be found on the lowered seventh degree, and the two chords will sound like a V–I progression in the relative major key.

EX. 347. Beethoven—*Sonata, op. 2, no. 1*

F: I   V$^6_5$ofIII   III   V$^6_5$ofIII   III   V   I^6 V I IV^6 V

VofIV

The major tonic triad actually stands in relation of dominant to the subdominant, although it needs the addition of a minor seventh to clarify this relationship to the hearer. This is one of the commonest of the secondary dominants and is very often used toward the end of a piece, where emphasis on the subdominant is desired to balance previous dominant modulations.

EX. 348. Mendelssohn—*String Quartet, op. 12*

B♭: I   V^{7}ofIV———————————— IV——— I

The subdominant is likewise frequently emphasized at the beginning of the movement by the use of VofIV, as in the example above from Beethoven's First Symphony and in the following:

EX. 349. Beethoven—*Prometheus: Overture*

C: V^{2}ofIV   IV^6 IV^6 V

EX. 350. Bach—*Well-tempered Clavier, I, Prelude no. 9*

F: I   V⁷ofIV   IV⁶₄   V/I   I

In an established minor mode it is, of course, necessary to raise the third degree chromatically to create the leading-tone of the sub-dominant.

EX. 351. Mozart—*Pianoforte Concerto, K. 466*

D: I⁶₄   V⁷   VI   V⁴₃ofIV   IV   II⁶₅   I⁶₄   V⁷

V of V

The dominant of the dominant has already been mentioned in connection with its use in half cadences (See Ex. 227). The following is a typical case in which a modulation to the dominant key would not be called for in the analysis. Note the use of a seventh in the final chord of a half cadence.

EX. 352. Schumann—*Slumber-song, op. 124, no. 16*

Allegretto

Eᵇ: II⁶   V⁶₅ofV   V⁷

In the following example the cross relation is to be remarked between the A-sharp, leading-tone of V, and the A-natural in the bass of the chord of resolution. This type of cross-relation is characterized by the fact that the first of the two notes is a leading-tone, which follows its tendency upward, while the lowered tone enters as a strong appoggiatura-like dissonance, with downward tendency, in the bass of a seventh chord in its third inversion.

EX. 353. Wagner—*Tannhäuser: Overture*

VofVI

Like the mediant, the submediant exists in major and minor form, with two dominants. The VofVI derived from the major scale is by far the more common of the two. In this chord the dominant of the key is chromatically raised.

EX. 354. Wagner—*Siegfried Idyll*

EX. 355. Schubert—*"Forellen" Quintet*

The original dominant of the key is not altered in the dominant harmony of the minor sixth degree, but its function changes from that of tonal degree to leading-tone. If the chord contains a seventh, a new tone—the chromatically lowered second degree—is introduced into the key.

EX. 356. Bruckner—*Symphony no. 7*

Unlike the mediant, the submediant of the minor mode is fairly common amid major harmonic surroundings. Its dominant seems rather remote from the major scale, as shown in Ex. 357.

VofVII

The leading-tone is not considered a possible temporary tonic, so that its dominant is not employed. The lowered melodic seventh degree of the minor scale can, however, be found attended by a dominant harmony. Used in connection with an established major mode, as in the following example, it demonstrates the coloristic possibilities of this interchangeability of the modes.

EX. 357. Bizet—*L'Arlésienne*

Formulae, to be played in all keys:

EXERCISES

1. Work out the following figured basses:

2. Construct a musical sentence of two phrases according to the following specifications:

a. The prevailing mode is minor; the meter is three-four; the rhythmic texture contains eighth-notes.

b. The first phrase modulates to the subdominant of the relative major.

c. The second phrase starts in that key and modulates to the original tonality.

d. The sentence ends with a plagal cadence introduced by VofIV and finishing with a "tierce de Picardie."

3. Harmonize the following unfigured basses:

Moderato

4. Harmonize the following soprano parts:

Fifteen | IRREGULAR RESOLUTIONS

THE regular resolution of the dominant seventh chord is to the tonic triad. Consequently all other resolutions are irregular. It is essential that the two aspects of irregular resolution be clearly appreciated before generalizations regarding the practice of composers can be made. The irregularity may consist in a departure from the customary practice in voice leading, or it may be a purely harmonic matter of root progression.

In the example below, the harmonic progression is typical of the regular resolution of a dominant seventh chord. V_7ofV proceeds to its tonic, V. On the other hand, the voice leading is as irregular as could be.

EX. 358. Schubert—*String Quartet, op. 29*

The progression V_7–VI is properly regarded as an irregular resolution, but the voice leading is almost certain to exemplify the rules for this progression.

EX. 359. Mendelssohn—*Andante, op. 82*

$$E^b: \quad II^6 \qquad I^6 \ V^7 \ VI \ IV \qquad I^6_4 \qquad V^7 \qquad I$$

The leading-tone moves to the tonic to emphasize the key. The second degree also moves to the tonic, as to ascend would form parallel fifths with the bass. The seventh of the chord resolves down, according to its tendency, but could not move up to the sixth degree as that would make a poor direct octave on the resolution of a dissonance.

It is customary to include the fifth in the V_7 chord in this progression. The V_7 in its incomplete form does not conveniently connect with VI, as the student may see by experiment.

EX. 360

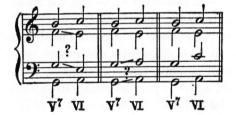

$$V^7 \ VI \qquad V^7 \ VI \qquad V^7 \ VI$$

The extra root can only move by the skip up to the tonic. Otherwise it would move either in parallel octaves with the bass, or to the direct octave with the resolution of the seventh.

The examples given show that a regular resolution may be made with extreme irregularity of melodic movement, whereas an irregular resolution may show strict regularity of voice leading.

All chord progressions are undoubtedly the product of melodic movement, as has been often stated; but since we are examining the practice of a particular period, in which it may be said that a vocabulary of chords exists, it seems reasonable to describe harmonic progressions in terms of root succession, considering as details the variants in form of the chords and the contrapuntal divergences.

Such a detail would be represented by the resolution of V_7 to V_7ofIV. The minor seventh above the tonic is in chromatic relationship with the leading-tone, so that usually the latter descends, although the cross-relation is sometimes used, especially when the lowered tone is in the bass.

EX. 361

V^7 V^7ofIV V^7 V^2ofIV

It is to be noted that when two seventh chords occur in succession one of them is usually incomplete, with doubled root. The melodic progression of the voices to the nearest position brings this about. Inversions of seventh chords are, however, almost always in complete form with all factors present. The above example shows a progression from a V_7 in root position to an inverted seventh chord. Hence the V_7 is constructed with doubled root so that the second chord will be completed naturally by the voice leading.

These two chords also show a dissonant chord resolving to another dissonant chord, an effect of frequent occurrence. One of the dissonant intervals, the minor seventh, resolves normally, while the other, the augmented fourth, moves in parallel motion to an equivalent dissonant interval, the diminished fifth. In all successions of dissonant chords it is important to notice the progression of the dissonant intervals.

In the following arrangement the chromatic bass is especially effective, and the minor third degree as passing tone gives the color of cross-relation with the leading-tone of the subdominant.

EX. 362. Bach—*Magnificat*

E: V^6_5 V^2ofIV

RESOLUTION TO THE SUPERTONIC

The supertonic triad makes a weak resolution for the dominant seventh, since it is in effect similar to a dominant ninth minus root and third. The seventh of V_7 is common to the two chords so it does not resolve. In the example, the presence of the seventh of II supplies a note of resolution for the leading-tone and thus strengthens the progression.

EX. 363. Brahms—*Intermezzo, op. 76, no. 3*

A^b: V^2 II^7

The alteration of II to VofV gives a more satisfactory chord of resolution, since the seventh may then proceed chromatically upward. In the following example the omission of the root in VofV eliminates another common tone.

The symbol V^0 will be used in this book to designate a dominant chord with root omitted.

EX. 364. Mozart—*Sonata, K. 533*

C:. I_4^6 V^7 V_6^0ofV

RESOLUTION TO THE MEDIANT

Chords on the third degree tend to become less independent when associated with dominant harmony. The major third degree sounds more like a nonharmonic melodic tone than like a real resolution of the seventh. The resolution to the major triad on the minor third degree is not often found.

EX. 365

Comparatively common as a chord of resolution, however, is the form of III which is dominant of the sixth degree. Here again there is a chromatic relationship involved.

EX. 366. Beethoven—*String Quartet, op. 18, no. 1*

RESOLUTION TO THE SUBDOMINANT

In the resolution to IV the seventh may be prolonged into the second chord (or repeated). When both chords are in root position, the leading-tone is placed in an inside voice, to avoid prominence of the cross-relation of the tritone.

EX. 367. Chopin—*Prelude, op. 28, no. 17*

More often the subdominant is found in first inversion, allowing a choice of doubling either tonic or fourth degree.

EX. 368

$$V^7 \quad IV^6 \qquad V^7 \quad IV^6$$

EX. 369. Mozart—*Sonata, K. 279*

$$F: II^6 \qquad I^6_4 \qquad V^7 \qquad IV^6 \qquad V^6_5 \qquad 1$$

RESOLUTION TO THE SUBMEDIANT

The voice leading in the V_7–VI progression, described in connection with Ex. 359, will of course be the same for the minor mode. In the following example the broken chords in the left-hand part stand for three sustained melodic parts. Hence in the V_7–VI progression A moves to G, D-sharp to E, and B to C. The eighth-note E in the right hand is an anticipation.

EX. 370. Rameau—*Gigue*

$$E: \quad I \qquad V^7 \qquad VI \qquad I^6$$

The example below, of V_7 resolving to V_7ofII, is unusual for its parallel motion. Also to be noticed is that the nonharmonic tones in the second and third measures outline the scale of G minor, the temporary tonality of the second degree of F major.

EX. 371. Mozart—*Sonata, K. 533*

An instance of the resolution of V_7 to VI_7, with root and third raised, may be seen in Ex. 238, from the Intermezzo by Brahms, op. 116, no. 6.

The examples given are by no means an exhaustive list of the irregular resolutions of V_7, even to the chords already studied. Excepting the mention of VI_7, chords not yet studied have not been used as illustrations. New chords will offer new resources in irregular resolutions, especially the diminished seventh chord.

The student is urged to experiment with resolutions of V_7, in root position and in inversion, to all chords in his vocabulary in a single tonality. Some will lend themselves poorly but the experience will show the degree of practicability of the various chords as possible resolutions.

THE SECONDARY DOMINANTS

The practice of irregular resolution is applicable to the secondary dominants, in a somewhat lesser scope. These chords are generally identified by their resolution to their temporary tonic. When such resolution is lacking it may be that a modulation has taken place, or that the chord appears as enharmonic notation of a chord of quite different harmonic significance, as for instance an augmented sixth chord. If, however, the resolution is to a chord unquestionably of the initial key, the secondary dominant is plainly understood as such, without weakening the tonality. The best example of this principle is the progression V_7ofVI to IV, which supports the original tonic better than the regular resolution by virtue of the tonal importance of the second chord.

EX. 372

VofVI   IV   II   V   I

As in the regular resolution, the secondary dominant and its chord
of resolution are considered temporarily in the key of the secondary
dominant for purposes of voice leading and doubling. Thus, in the
example above, V_7ofVI to IV is identical with V_7 to VI in the key
of VI, here A minor, so the voice leading is carried out as in V_7–VI,
resulting in the doubling of A, a tonal degree in the key of VI, but
a modal degree in the main key of C. The same voice leading is seen
in the example below, with the two chords in first inversion.

EX. 373. Bach—*Chorale: Nun lob' mein' Seel' den Herren*

C: V_5^6ofVI IV⁶   I V^7 VI I_4^6 V^7 I

In the following example, V_7ofVI is approached from V, with tenor
and bass moving in parallel fifths and the voices overlapping. The
subsequent resolution is perfectly orthodox.

EX. 374. Cherubini—*Anacreon Overture*

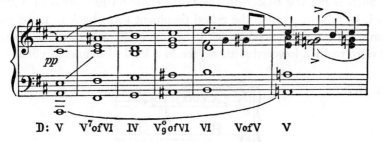

D: V V^7ofVI   IV V_9^oofVI   VI   VofV   V

The same relationship is found between V_7ofIII and its irregular
resolution to I. Analysis as an appoggiatura chord is ordinarily possible, or the chord may result from other melodic tones, such as the

auxiliary used in several voices. In Ex. 375, tenor and bass, here viola and 'cello, move in parallel octaves to effect the resolution, with a momentary change to three-part texture.

EX. 375. Beethoven—*String Quartet, op. 18, no. 5*

D: V^{o}_{2} of VI   VI V^{7} of III   I V^{7} I

The dominant of the supertonic progresses quite naturally to V_7, the altered tonic following its tendency as leading-tone of the second degree.

EX. 376. Franck—*Symphony*

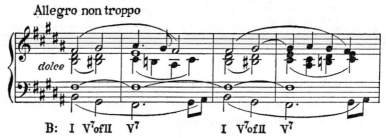

B: I V^{7} of II V^{7} I V^{7} of II V^{7}

Such is not the case with the fairly common resolution of V_7 of VI to I. In this progression the raised dominant turns back to its original form, not a usual procedure with chromatic alteration. It is as though it were really a lowered sixth degree in a kind of dominant effect.

EX. 377

V^{4}_{3} of VI $\left(\overset{v}{?}\right)$ I

EX. 378. Schubert—*Sonata, op. 53*

Among the irregular resolutions of V₇ofV, that to the triad on the third degree is a similar progression of V₇ofVI going to IV, and V₇ of III going to I. The voice leading produces a doubled third in the chord of resolution.

EX. 379. Chopin—*Mazurka, op. 7, no. 4*

With the resolution of a secondary dominant to another secondary dominant, the validity of the harmonic functions in tonality is demonstrated. The chords as dominants represent degrees of the key, but each contains at least one note foreign to the scale. It will be readily appreciated that the secondary dominants are a source of much harmonic enrichment and a remarkable extension of the unity of a single tonal center. The following are two examples out of numerous possibilities.

EX. 380. Schubert—*Quintet, op. 163*

EX. 381. Franck—*Prelude, Aria, and Finale*

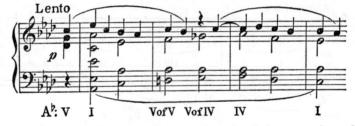

The student should try resolutions of each of the secondary dominants to the various chords in a key, translating the progressions into terms of the tonality of the secondary dominant to clarify the voice leading.

The irregular resolutions vary widely in the frequency of their use. Only by the continued experience of observation of the circumstances affecting their employment by composers can knowledge of the practice be acquired. It is suggested that examples of the resolutions be collected gradually as they are seen in actual music, and that the student play them in all keys until their individual characteristics are assimilated, at the same time attempting to classify each as to its commonness or rarity.

Formulae, to be played in all keys:

Formulae of resolutions of secondary dominants are not given, as they would differ from the above only in the analysis. For example, V₇–VI in C would be exactly like V₇ofIII–I in A-flat, V₇ofVI–IV in E-flat, etc.

EXERCISES

1. Write four irregular resolutions of each of the following chords: E-flat V_7; E-flat minor V_7ofIV; F major V_7ofVI; C minor $V_7$of V.

2. Write single phrases according to the following harmonic schemes:

    a. D major, I–V_7ofIV–IV–I–V_7ofII–II–V_7–I.

    b. E minor, V_7–V_7ofIV–IV–I–V_7ofV–V_7–I.

    c. A-flat major, I–V_7–IV–V_7ofVI–VI–V_7ofV–I–V_7–I.

    d. G major, I–V_7ofIII–V_7ofVI–V_7ofII–V_7ofV–V_7–I.

3. Work out the following figured basses:

4. Harmonize the following soprano parts:

Andante

5. Harmonize the following basses:

c

Sixteen | THE DIMINISHED SEVENTH CHORD

WITH the superposition of another third upon the dominant seventh chord, the group of chords known as dominant harmony is extended to include two dominant ninth chords, major and minor.

EX. 382

The dominant ninth chords are most often found with root omitted, their dominant implication being sufficiently strong whether or not the actual fifth degree is present. Composers have shown a distinct preference for the incomplete forms of these chords over the comparatively thick and heavy effect of the ninth chord with root.

Dominant harmony consists, then, of the following group of chords:

EX. 383

$$V \quad V^7 \quad V^o_7 \quad V^9 \quad V^o_9 \quad V^{9\flat} \quad V^o_{9\flat}$$

By far the commonest of the dominant ninths is the last of the group shown in the example, the incomplete dominant minor ninth, known as the diminished seventh chord. The intervals making up this chord are minor third, diminished fifth, and diminished seventh. Examination of these intervals will show the dissonant characteristics of the chord.

When it is arranged as a series of thirds, its lowest tone is the leading-tone, which, in addition to its inherent tendency, is found to be in dissonant interval-relationship to the fifth and seventh. (Note that the terms "fifth" and "seventh" are here applied to the chord as a seventh chord on the leading-tone. Those factors would be the "seventh" and "ninth" of the original ninth chord. It would, however, be illogical to refer to the leading-tone as "root" of the chord.)

The third, the second degree, forms with the sixth degree a diminished fifth, so that all the factors of this chord are involved in dissonant relationships.

EX. 384

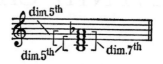

A chord made up entirely of tendency tones would seem to be a chord of very definite tonal significance, but, paradoxically, the diminished seventh chord is the most ambiguous of chords. The thirds are all minor thirds, and the inversion of the diminished seventh, the augmented second, is the equivalent of the minor third under our tempered scale system. The diminished fifth interval has likewise an equivalent sound in its inversion, the augmented fourth. In consequence the ear cannot distinguish the factors of a diminished seventh chord until its resolution shows which is the leading-tone, etc. The chord and its inversions have the same sound harmonically.

EX. 385

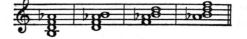

ENHARMONIC EQUIVALENTS

By application of the enharmonic principle, the same diminished seventh chord can be written in four different ways, taking each note in turn as leading-tone.

EX. 386

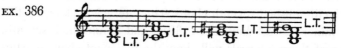

The leading-tone is readily found in each case by arranging the chord in a series of thirds, when it will appear as the lowest tone.

Such changes in notation, by designation of the leading-tone, mean change of tonality and also change of root of the chord. The root is found a major third below the leading-tone. It is interesting to observe that the four roots of one diminished seventh chord in its enharmonic changes form in themselves the arpeggio of another diminished seventh chord.

EX. 387

C: V   E♭: V   F♯: V   A: V

Players of stringed instruments know that these different interpretations of one chord involve an actual change of pitch. The note A-flat with destination G is perceptibly lower than the leading-tone G-sharp with destination A. It is likewise the experience of many musical persons that the pitch of the notes seems actually to change when the different roots are struck in the bass against a diminished seventh chord sustained on the pianoforte.

EX. 388

RESOLUTION

The regular resolution of the diminished seventh chord, as an incomplete dominant ninth, is to the tonic triad. It is customary to resolve the two intervals of the diminished fifth, contracting each to a third, without regard for the doubling that results. If the diminished fifth is inverted, the augmented fourth will, of course, expand to a sixth. The diminished seventh chord resolves with equal frequency to either a major or a minor tonic.

EX. 389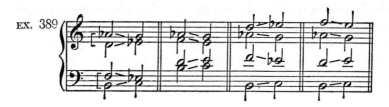

The augmented fourth may, however, abandon its natural resolution so that the three upper voices will descend in parallel motion. Such procedure is not followed if the interval is a diminished fifth, which would then approach the perfect fifth by similar motion.

EX. 390

accepted   accepted   avoided

EX. 391. Bach—*Chorale: Es ist das Heil*

E: I   I⁶   {E:IV   V   V⁰₉ I   V
                     {F#:VI

INVERSIONS

As shown above, in Ex. 385, the inversions of the diminished seventh chord and the position with the leading tone in the bass all sound alike harmonically. They vary contrapuntally in the orientation of the factors, the bass being especially important; but this is realized by the hearer only through the manner of resolution.

Since the root of the chord is not present, there can be no root position, strictly speaking, although the grouping in which the leading-tone is the lowest tone is often called root position. In this book the symbol V⁰₉ will be used for this position. For the inversions the V will be used to indicate a dominant root which is not present in the chord, and the Arabic numerals will show the intervals formed between the bass and the upper voices.

EX. 392

These "inversions" resolve in the same way as the root position. When the second degree is in the bass it usually resolves to the third degree to avoid a direct fifth on the resolution of the diminished fifth.

EX. 393

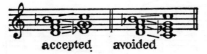

accepted   avoided

The six-four-three inversion, with the subdominant in the bass, ordinarily resolves to the first inversion of the tonic triad, but it may also resolve to root position.

EX. 394

When the lower tone is the ninth, or submediant, the natural resolution is to the tonic six-four chord, which means dominant followed by dominant, a rhythmically weak progression. Furthermore the disposition of the voices will be likely to produce a doubling of the sixth or the fourth in the chord of resolution. This grouping is, therefore, less useful than the others.

EX. 395

As a rule, in four-part writing no factor of a diminished seventh chord is omitted in any position.

THE SECONDARY DOMINANTS

The diminished seventh chord is employed as a secondary dominant wherever such chords are used, whether the temporary tonic is major or minor. The following examples show some of the secondary dominants in the form of diminished sevenths.

EX. 396. Brahms—*Intermezzo, op. 76, no. 7*

EX. 397. Brahms—*Waltz, op. 39, no. 3*

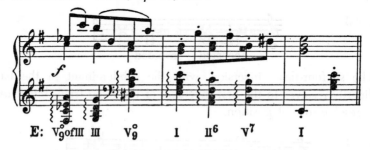

EX. 398. Bach—*Well-tempered Clavier, II, Prelude no. 12*

EX. 399. Bach—*B-minor Mass: Kyrie*

EX. 400. Schumann—*Pianoforte Concerto*

EX. 401. Mozart—*Quintet, K. 406*

EX. 402. Haydn—*String Quartet, op. 76, no. 1*

IRREGULAR RESOLUTION

Since it is the resolution that establishes the tonal identity of the diminished seventh chord, most apparently irregular resolutions will be discovered to be regular when the notation of the diminished seventh chord is revised. Composers have never been overscrupulous as to the grammatical notation of this chord, especially in writing for keyboard instruments, so that the student must be prepared to judge the chord by what it does rather than by its appearance on paper.

EX. 403. Chopin—*Waltz, op. 64, no. 3*

Moderato

A^b: I $V^o_6 \text{ of V}$ V^6_5 I

In the above example the E-double-flat should be written as D-natural, leading-tone of the dominant. The harmonic resolution is regular (VofV to V) but the melodic resolution of the D down to D-flat is irregular, although not uncommon.

The following is cited in a harmonic treatise as an instance of irregular resolution of a diminished seventh chord:

EX. 404

In this case the B-natural has no leading-tone function relative to the second chord. If it were written C-flat the true nature of the two chords would be clear. They are both derived from the same root B-flat, the ninth C-flat resolving into the B-flat, so there is no harmonic resolution.

EX. 405

$E^{\natural}$: V————

Although detailed study will have to await a later chapter, it is necessary to call attention to two diminished seventh chords which do not fall in the category of dominants. They are II₇ and VI₇ with root and third chromatically raised, acting as appoggiatura chords to I and V₇ respectively.

EX. 406

II⁷   I⁶   VI⁷   V⁶₅

Like other diminished sevenths these two chords are identified by their resolutions. They are mentioned here to avoid confusion with irregular resolutions and incorrect notations of other chords.

The diminished seventh chord will seldom be found without either the dominant relationship to its chord of resolution, or a relationship such as the two shown above. Only if these are lacking can the resolution be called irregular harmonically, in terms of root progression.

EX. 407. Mendelssohn—*Midsummer Night's Dream: Notturno*

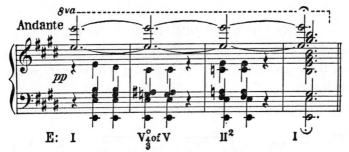

Often the chord preceding the diminished seventh, or the general sense of tonality, will give it a meaning other than that defined by the resolution. The effect may be explained as irregular resolution, or as enharmonic change in the chord.

EX. 408. Rameau—*The Hen*

Irregularity of voice leading is common practice in the treatment of the diminished seventh chord. Voices are allowed to move freely among the chord tones, over such "unmelodic" intervals as the augmented second and fourth, diminished fifth and seventh. It should be remembered, however, that these are really instrumental voices.

EX. 409. Schubert—*Symphony no. 5*

CONSECUTIVE DIMINISHED SEVENTHS

Sequences of more than two diminished sevenths are often employed, the vagueness of the chord causing a momentary uncertainty of tonality.

EX. 410. Beethoven—*Sonata, op. 10, no. 3*

EX. 411. Beethoven—*Pianoforte Concerto no. 4*

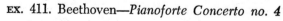

In rapid harmonic movement, successive diminished sevenths progressing by half step in similar motion give the effect of chromatic passing tones, although the chords are related harmonically. In the following example the parallel movement is disguised by the changes of position in the right-hand part. Each chord may be considered a dominant of the next, with some enharmonic revision. In actual performance the ear grasps as harmony only the first and last chords of the group.

EX. 412. Chopin—*Etude, op. 10, no. 3*

MODULATION

The tonal ambiguity of the diminished seventh chord is turned to versatility when it is a question of modulation. This versatility is unmatched by any other chord. A single diminished seventh chord, without enharmonic change, is capable, like any dominant chord, of the following analyses: V, VofII, VofIII (in min.), VofIII (in maj.), VofIV, VofV, VofVI (in min.), VofVI (in maj.), VofVII (in min.). Add to these the nondominant forms II_7 and VI_7, and the dominant of the lowered second degree (V_9^0 of N_6), and we have twelve interpretations for the one chord. Moreover, since the chord may be enharmonically written in four different ways without changing the sound, we may multiply the above by four, making a total of forty-eight possible interpretations.

There are, however, certain limitations upon the usefulness of the diminished seventh as an effective pivot chord in modulation. To begin with, it is not advisable to employ the dominant of the new key as a pivot chord, the chord before it being a better common ground between the two keys. Further, if a secondary dominant is selected, it may happen that its chord of resolution is still a good chord in the first key and would be a more logical pivot chord than the diminished seventh.

EX. 413

In the above example, the modulation may be effected in theory by the diminished seventh chord; but actually its chord of resolution is the real pivot chord, as it is both I in A and II in G, and it introduces the dominant of the new key. If we wish to use V_9^o of A as pivot chord in a modulation to G it is better to assume an enharmonic change (G-sharp = A-flat), making the dominant of IV in G. By resolving to the minor form of IV the key of A is excluded from the harmony following the diminished seventh chord.

EX. 414

Formulae, to be played in all keys:

EXERCISES

1. Correct the notation of the following diminished seventh chords, to agree with the resolutions given.

2. Work out in four parts the following figured basses:

3. Interpret the following chord in the keys named, using enharmonic change when necessary, and showing the resolution of the chord in each key.

Keys: G, A-flat, B-flat, C, E.

4. Construct a phrase using four diminished seventh chords in succession.

5. Harmonize the following melodies, introducing diminished seventh chords:

6. Harmonize the following unfigured basses, introducing diminished seventh chords:

Seventeen | THE INCOMPLETE MAJOR NINTH

THE seventh chord constructed on the leading-tone and using the major mode bears a striking contrast to that from the minor mode, the diminished seventh. These chords are both dominant ninths without root, and they both resolve regularly to the tonic triad but they are different in several respects.

Whereas in the diminished seventh chord the intervals between the factors were the same, and enharmonically equivalent in the inversions, the use of the major sixth degree gives a major third between the two upper factors. This causes a marked difference in the character of the inversions.

EX. 415

The last inversion (ninth in the bass) is rarely found except as a dominant seventh chord in which the sixth degree appears as a suspension in the bass, resolving to the root. Indeed, a tendency is noticeable throughout the period of harmonic common practice to treat the upper tone of the major ninth interval, with or without root, as a melodic tone, resolving it to the tone below before the resolution of the chord takes place. The very characteristic sonority of the major ninth, however, makes a harmonic effect, especially when the leading-tone is present and the chord is in root position.

EX. 416. Schubert—*Sonata, op. 120*

In the resolution, the presence of the perfect fifth between second and sixth degrees may lead to parallel fifths in the voice leading. This is usually avoided by moving the second degree up to the third or by skip of a fifth down to the dominant. In neither case will the root be doubled in the tonic triad.

EX. 417

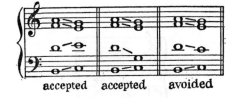

If the upper voices are so arranged that the interval of a fifth is inverted to a fourth, all three may descend in parallel motion. This contrapuntal advantage has, however, not been valued above the typical sound of the major ninth when heard in the top voice. Compare the sonority of the following with the disposition shown above.

EX. 418. Bach—*Chorale: Jesu, nun sei gepreiset*

EX. 419

In the example below, the instrumental writing creates actually seven melodic parts, hence the direct fifth in the resolution, between the two lower voices.

EX. 420. Dvořák—*String Quartet, op. 96*

The six-five-three inversion must resolve to the first inversion of the tonic chord to avoid parallel fifths between the bass and the resolution of the ninth.

EX. 421

The following resolution is like the above. The apparent multiplicity of parts is due mainly to instrumental octave doublings. Parallel octaves are the result of this reduplication and are not defects of voice leading.

EX. 422. Mendelssohn—*Midsummer Night's Dream: Overture*

The six-four-three inversion is more useful as there are more alternative possibilities of its arrangement. It may resolve to either root position or first inversion.

EX. 423

EX. 424. Haydn—*Sonata*

B♭: V of VI VI   V°₄₃   I

EX. 425. Grieg—*Lyric Piece, op. 43, no. 1*

A: V°₄₃   I⁶

Unlike the diminished seventh chord, this chord is not equally appropriate to both modes. The major sixth degree as a dissonance tends to descend, which it could not normally do in the minor scale, without undue prominence of the cross-relation of the tritone between sixth and third degrees. If the sixth degree were purely melodic, it could ascend as a step of the melodic minor scale but would lose its harmonic significance as a ninth.

EX. 426

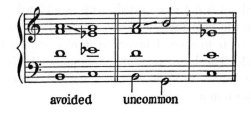

avoided   uncommon

IRREGULAR RESOLUTION

The incomplete major ninth is not capable of greatly varied resolution. The progression to supertonic harmony is weak because all the tones of II are common to both chords.

In the resolution to III the chord loses its identity as a dominant ninth without root and becomes a seventh chord on the leading-tone (VII$_7$). This progression is most often seen in harmonic sequences.

EX. 427. Brahms—*Ballade, op. 118, no. 3*

Resolutions to IV may be made, but if the subdominant chord has the tonic in the bass there is really a regular resolution in disguise.

EX. 428

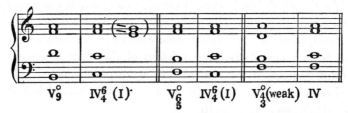

The submediant is not more satisfactory as a chord of resolution. If the tonic is in the bass the VI chord is really I (regular resolution). If the VI chord is in second inversion it represents III, and the V$_9^0$ is really a VII$_7$. The latter nondominant quality is likewise strongly felt in the progression to VI in root position, the two chords sounding like II–I in the minor mode.

EX. 429

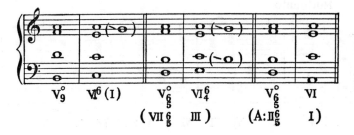

THE SECONDARY DOMINANTS

The incomplete dominant major ninth is far less useful as a secondary dominant than the diminished seventh chord. This is due to its inability to act as dominant of a minor tonic. It is, for instance, inaccurate to refer to the chord of resolution in the following deceptive cadence by Chopin as VofII. The dominant ninth of the supertonic is properly a minor ninth and the use here of the very rare seventh chord on the raised tonic heightens the deceptive quality of the cadence.

EX. 430. Chopin—*Prelude, op. 28, no. 2*

The degrees which may be preceded by a major ninth are, then, in the major mode I, IV, V, and in the minor mode III, V, VI. In the case of III, its dominant in this form would be identical with the seventh chord on the second degree.

EX. 431

The dominant of the subdominant with major ninth resolves to the major form of IV.

EX. 432. Mozart—*String Quartet, K. 458*

Most common of the secondary dominants in this form is V_9^0 of V.

EX. 433. Franck—*Symphony*

V_9^0 of V may be found in irregular resolution, of which the following are two examples.

EX. 434. Brahms—*Capriccio, op. 116, no. 3*

EX. 435. Schubert—*Sonata, op. 164*

MODULATION

From the foregoing it will be evident that the incomplete dominant major ninth offers somewhat limited opportunities as a pivot chord in modulation. There are no possibilities of enharmonic change as with the diminished seventh chord. The interpretations of the V_9^0 chord of the key of C are these: VofIV in G major; VofV in F; VofVI in E; II_7 in A.

Formulae, to be played in all keys:

USE OF OPEN SCORE

Students who have acquired a knowledge of the various clefs should write all exercises on four staves, using the appropriate clefs for the different parts. Others should begin practice in reading the C-clefs and should start the habit of working out the exercises in open score. Emphasis should be placed upon the value of this practice for gaining facility in score reading. Obviously there is little point in writing the exercise first in close score (two staves) and then copying it on four staves.

Apart from the mechanical benefits of practice, writing in open score calls attention to the linear structure of the music, each voice being more readily apparent as a melodic and rhythmic line.

For those unfamiliar with any but treble and bass clefs it is suggested that the disposition of the string quartet be used at first.

EX. 436

When this combination can be read with a fair degree of ease, the alto clef may be shifted to the alto voice and a tenor clef used for the tenor part.

EX. 437

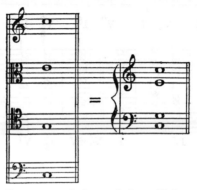

Finally, the combination of four clefs will be achieved by substituting the soprano clef for the treble clef. This is the normal arrangement found in standard complete editions such as the Bach-Gesellschaft edition, so that ability to read the clefs and score becomes a practical necessity.

EX. 438

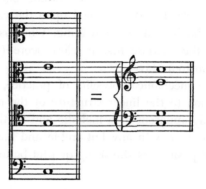

Other clefs may be used for practice, provided the objective of the study of harmony is not lost sight of in the process. The mezzo-soprano and baritone clefs are useful in transposition and are occasionally seen in the published works of composers.

EXERCISES

1. Construct three separate original phrases, illustrating three different modulations in which the pivot chord is the incomplete dominant major ninth of the first key.

2. Work out the following figured basses:

3. Harmonize the following melodies, using the Chord V_9^0 and its inversions where appropriate:

4. Harmonize the following basses:

Eighteen | THE COMPLETE DOMINANT NINTH

F AR less frequently employed than the incomplete forms is the complete dominant ninth chord in its two forms, major and minor.

EX. 439

Reduction of this chord of five factors to four-part writing necessitates omission of one factor, which is usually the fifth. The fifth is unimportant contrapuntally compared to the other chord members as it has no strong tendency and the characteristic sound of the dominant ninth seems unaffected by its omission.

The regular resolution of the chord would then take place as follows:

EX. 440

In practice, however, it is rare that the voices do not contain some melodic movement in the course of which all the factors of the chord may be touched upon.

Treatment of the complete dominant ninth chord by composers of the eighteenth and nineteenth centuries has three important aspects:

1. The ninth may appear as any of the types of nonharmonic

217

melodic tones, resolving into the fifth degree before the chord itself resolves. It is often an appoggiatura, in which case the harmonic color is very pronounced, but even when it is rhythmically weak its harmonic significance is recognized by the ear.

EX. 441. Brahms—*Intermezzo, op. 76, no. 3*

EX. 442. Bach—*Well-tempered Clavier, II, Fugue no. 5*

2. The ninth may be used in a true harmonic sense as a chord tone but it may be absent from the chord at the moment of change of harmony. This is an important aspect of harmonic treatment of the ninth fairly common in the classics. It actually means the non-resolution of a dissonant factor, a principle applied in common practice to no other dissonant chord. It is as though the ninth were regarded as an overtone in the dominant sonority, too high in the series to need to take part in the resolution effected by the seventh of the chord. Such treatment of the ninth implies a slowly moving root progression in comparison with the melodic activity.

EX. 443. Mozart—*Symphony, K. 550*

EX. 444. Beethoven—*Pianoforte Concerto, op. 37*

EX. 445. Beethoven—*String Quartet, op. 18, no. 1*

EX. 446. Schubert—*Mass in E-flat: Kyrie*

3. Lastly, the ninth may act as a normal dissonant chord tone resolving to a tone of the following chord.

EX. 447. Franck—*Sonata for Violin and Piano*

EX. 448. Beethoven—*Symphony no. 3*

In the example below the voice leading is more or less lost in the pianoforte pedal effect. The resolution of the ninth chord is accompanied by a dynamic change from loud to *dolcissimo,* as well as a change of register and of movement.

EX. 449. Liszt—*Sonette 47 del Petrarca*

The above excerpts show the minor ninth resolving to either a major or a minor tonic. The major ninth, complete or incomplete, is used only before the major tonic.

The major dominant ninth has further limitations with respect to the common practice of composers. It represents a harmonic color and style of the end of the common-practice period rather than of the eighteenth century. Employed as in the third of the three aspects described above it cannot be said to be of frequent use until the latter part of the nineteenth century. The isolated instances of parallel-moving ninth chords should certainly not be mentioned as examples of harmonic common practice, but should be noted as exceptional cases of a procedure to be exploited in a later period.

PREPARATION

Dominant ninth chords, like all chords of dominant harmony, are introduced with or without preparation.

SPACING

When the root of the ninth chord is present, and the chord is used in the usual harmonic sense (aspect three), care is taken to place the ninth at least a ninth above the root. It is practically never found below the root and preference is shown for the arrangement of the chord in which the leading-tone is below, rather than above, the ninth.

It is, of course, possible to place the factors close together, all within the range of an octave. In a chord which contains all but two of the seven tones of the scale the effect of this is not of a ninth chord, but more that of a chord built with intervals of a second, or what is known in the twentieth century as a "tone-cluster."

EX. 450

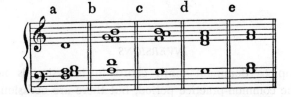

Considering the above dispositions: a. is not heard as a ninth chord; b. is usually avoided since the root is higher than the ninth; c. has more of the characteristic sound of the dominant ninth chord although not ideal, as the ninth is below the leading-tone; d. shows the importance of the leading-tone, by its omission, in the typical ninth chord sound; e. is the most usual arrangement. It will prove instructive to the student to play these chords and note carefully their comparative harmonic effect.

The peculiarly strident sound of the following minor ninth chord is largely due to the spacing, as well as to the placing of the root D close to the ninth E-flat.

EX. 451. Beethoven—*Symphony no. 9*

The root may appear above the minor ninth in a nonharmonic function as appoggiatura to the seventh. This effect is not uncommon and sh̶o̶ ̶ ̶ be regarded as a diminished seventh chord, the root nonharm̶

EX. 452. Chopin—*Mazurka, op. 56, no. 3*

INVERSIONS

The complete dominant ninth chord in inversion is not often found in the common-practice period, but there are occasional examples. It is important that the spacing in the inversions follow the restrictions regarding the relative positions of ninth, root, and leading-tone, if the characteristic sonority of the chord is desired.

In figuring basses for the inversions the spacing is not taken into account, the Arabic numerals simply identifying the notes to be used in arranging the chord.

EX. 453

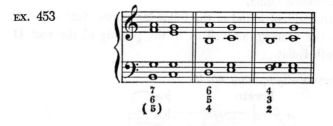

The fourth inversion is not used as that would place the ninth below the root. The second inversion, with the fifth in the bass, is less used than the other two.

EX. 454. Lalo—*Spanish Symphony*

EX. 455. Haydn—*Sonata*

IRREGULAR RESOLUTION

The student should experiment with the connection of V_9 to other chords in the key, judging the result both contrapuntally and for its harmonic effect. Irregular resolutions found in the works of composers should likewise be noted. These successions cannot always be called resolutions because the ninth may be unresolved or treated nonharmonically. A few examples are here given.

EX. 456. Haydn—*String Quartet, op. 64, no. 2*

EX. 457. Franck—*Symphonic Variations*

$F^\sharp$: V^9 IV^6 $V^o_6$of$V$$VI^6$ V I

EX. 458. Schubert—*Sonata, op. 122*

$E^\flat$: V^7 I^6 V^9 VI

EX. 459. Liszt—*Sonata*

E: V^9 $F^\sharp$:$\begin{cases} II^7 \\ V^o_9 of II \ II \end{cases}$ I^6

SECONDARY DOMINANTS

The complete ninth chord is used as a secondary dominant, the limitation being that the major ninth is not used to introduce a minor tonic. Irregular resolutions of secondary dominant ninths are occasionally employed, as in the following example:

EX. 460. Wagner—*Die Meistersinger, Act III*

Below are further examples of the ninth chord as a secondary dominant.

EX. 461. Chopin—*Nocturne, op. 72, no. 1*

EX. 462. Bach—*Well-tempered Clavier, I, Prelude no. 12*

EX. 463. Franck—*Symphony*

EX. 464. Moussorgsky—*Death's Serenade*

E♭: I   II⁶   I   V⁹ofIII   III   V

MODULATION

The ninth chord has the disadvantage of all dominant chords in modulation in that the pivot chord is preferably not the dominant of the new key. It is, therefore, more effectively used as a secondary dominant in the second key, or even in both. Irregular resolution of the pivot chord is an added resource. The presence of the root takes away the possibilities of enharmonic change which were so numerous in the incomplete minor ninth chord.

In the following example, the ninth chord appears as the chord of resolution in the deceptive cadence in D. Hence it is taken as the pivot chord in the sudden modulation to B-flat, in order that the formula of the deceptive cadence may be preserved in the analysis.

EX. 465. Franck—*Symphony*

D: VofV   II(f♮=e♯)   VofIV   II   VofV   V   V⁹ofVI
                                                     B♭:V   I

Formulae, to be played in all keys:

V⁹   I   V⁹   I   V⁹   I   V⁷₆   I   V⁶₅₄   I⁶

$$V^9 \quad V^0_9 \text{of VI} \quad VI \quad V^9 \text{of V} \quad V^7 \quad V^9 \text{of IV} \quad V^9 \quad V^0_9 \text{of II} \quad V^0_9 \quad I$$

EXERCISES

1. Work out the following figured basses:

2. Construct original phrases showing the treatment of the dominant ninth chord in the following three ways:

    a. With the ninth as a melodic nonharmonic tone

    b. With the ninth as an unresolved harmonic factor

    c. With the ninth as a normal harmonic dissonance

3. Write in four parts the following progressions:

    a. E-flat: V_9–$V_9$of II

    b. G: $V_9$of II–$V_9$of V

    c. A: $V_9\flat$–$V_9\flat$of V

    d. F major: $V_9$of VI–IV

    e. B-flat: V_9–VI

4. Construct a phrase modulating from G major to F major, in

which the pivot chord is a major ninth chord, secondary dominant in both keys.

5. Harmonize the following unfigured basses, introducing complete dominant ninth chords:

6. Harmonize the following melodies, introducing complete dominant ninth chords:

Nineteen | THE SEQUENCE

THE harmonic sequence, the systematic transposition of a melodic, rhythmic, and harmonic pattern, is a resource of development in music. The change of pitch adds the element of variety to the unity of repetition. While the sequence may readily become a refuge for the composer of lesser talent, it has been used with great effectiveness by the best composers. It is often on close analysis discovered to be the basis for many passages which do not at first seem sequential, notably in the fugue and in symphonic developments and transitional sections.

We are here concerned primarily with the harmonic background of the various kinds of sequence and will give our attention to those sequences which do not attempt to conceal their fundamental structure.

THE INITIAL PATTERN

The pattern chosen for systematic transposition in the sequence may be of a variety of forms. Its length may vary from a single short motive on a single chord to a whole phrase. Although it is possible to construct a pattern of musical significance with but one chord as background, this kind of pattern is less interesting harmonically and the sequence is mainly dependent for its effect on the contrapuntal arrangement.

EX. 466. Beethoven—*Trio, op. 1, no. 3*

C: I   VI   IV   II

Most often the pattern contains two chords. In the following example they are simple triads with roots a fourth apart, the commonest strong progression.

EX. 467. Mozart—*Sonata for Two Pianofortes, K. 448*

A: I   IV   II   V   III   VI   IV   I

If the pattern is of much length it is not so readily recognized as sequential as the shorter group, which can be heard as a unit. A short phrase may be successfully used as pattern in a sequence.

EX. 468. Beethoven—*Sonata, op. 10, no. 1*

HARMONIC RHYTHM

The harmonic formula upon which the pattern is based has its rhythmic form, arising from the choice of root progressions, time values, and other contributing elements. Example 467 shows a simple rhythm of strong to weak in the pattern. In Ex. 468 the rhythm is strong-weak-weak-strong. If the rhythmic pattern begins with an anacrusis a more fluent sequence will result.

EX. 469. Beethoven—*Sonata, op. 106*

The anacrusis may be strong enough to give the effect of syncopation in the melodic rhythms. It should be noted in the following example that the harmonic rhythm is in agreement with the meter, whereas the preponderance of melodic rhythmic stress is on the third beat of the measure.

EX. 470. Mozart—*Quintet, K. 593*

The rhythmic impression of pressing forward is heightened if the anacrusis is long, followed by a short down-beat.

EX. 471. Brahms—*Intermezzo, op. 10, no. 3*

LENGTH OF THE SEQUENCE

It is generally agreed that a single transposition of the pattern does not constitute a sequence, the systematic transposition not being established until the third appearance of the initial group. On the other hand, it is remarkable that composers seldom allow the symmetry to extend beyond the third appearance of the pattern without breaking it up by variation or abandoning it altogether. This rule may be stated as an observation without presuming to deduce a principle of aesthetics therefrom.

Exceptions to the above rule may of course be found, and in certain types of musical expression, such as virtuoso cadenzas and compositions intended for technical study or display, sequences are sometimes written to extend by numerous repetitions throughout the entire range of the instrument.

DEGREE OF TRANSPOSITION

The pattern may be transposed by any interval, up or down. The interval chosen depends upon two factors, the desired harmonic destination of the sequential passage, and the feasibility of the connection of the pattern to itself when transposed. Construction of a sequence necessitates consideration of both of these problems.

THE NONMODULATING SEQUENCE

The sequence is either a modulating sequence, changing the tonal center with each transposition of the pattern, or a nonmodulating sequence, sometimes called a tonal sequence, with one tonal center throughout.

In the nonmodulating sequence the transpositions are made to degrees of the scale of the key. This causes some variation in the pattern since the intervals between the degrees of the scale are not always the same. For instance, in Ex. 467 the harmonic background is as follows: I–IV, II–V, III–VI. The initial pattern consists of two major triads, the second of a minor and a major triad, and the third of two minor triads. Note that the transposition is upwards the interval of a major second, while the root progression at the joint between the patterns is down a minor third.

The nonmodulating sequence is likely to contain variation, too, in the interval of transposition of the pattern. In Ex. 469 the first transposition is down a minor third, while the second is down a major third, resulting from the intervals between I, VI, and IV in the major scale.

Both of these variations are present in the sequence shown below, descending by seconds. The root progressions are by fourths throughout the entire passage, all perfect fourths except from VI to II.

EX. 472. Paradisi—*Sonata*

SECONDARY DOMINANTS

The employment of secondary dominants in the nonmodulating sequence adds the harmonic color of tones foreign to the scale of the main tonality, contributes the rhythmic element of dissonance, and emphasizes the unity of the group of chords comprising the pattern.

EX. 473. Beethoven—*Sonata, op. 7*

B^b: VofVI VI   VofIV IV   VofII II   I$^6_4$ V   I

The following short sequence shows roots in progression by perfect fourths throughout, at one-beat time intervals. The secondary dominants with their resolutions divide the harmonic rhythm into a meter of two-four against the prevailing three-four meter.

EX. 474. Chopin—*Mazurka, op. 24, no. 3*

A^b: VofIII III   VofII II   V I

Sequences in which each harmony is a dominant of the next are of uncertain tonality and may or may not be felt as being in a single key.

EX. 475. A. Scarlatti—*Fugue*

B^b: VofII VofV   V(ofI) VofIV VofVII VofIII   VofVI VI   II
or F: VofV V   E^{b}VofV V   D^{b}VofV V

In the following sequence the secondary dominant is not used on the third appearance of the pattern because the supertonic triad in minor, being a diminished triad, does not act as a temporary tonic.

EX. 476. Haydn—*String Quartet, op. 76, no. 4*

Some sequences give the impression of a unity of tonality while employing harmonies even more suggestive of temporary tonal centers than are the secondary dominants. The prominent harmonic feature in the example below is undoubtedly the sense of a strong half cadence in the keys of B, A, and D. The subdominant character of the first chord in each group is not taken into account by its analysis as a plain triad in the fundamental key. This suggests the possibility of extension of the secondary dominant principle to other secondary tonal functions. II of D is used here as IVofVI, and I as IVofV.

EX. 477. Mozart—*Menuetto, K. 355*

When the temporary tonics are themselves unsatisfactory chords of the main tonality, the impression of modulation is given, although in many cases these modulations are so fleeting that even a far-fetched explanation of the relationship of the chord to the main key is preferable. In the following example two analyses are offered. The first is nonmodulating, but necessitates reference to the minor triad on the dominant and the triad on the lowered seventh degree as temporary tonics. The second, on the other hand, shows four changes of tonal center in as many measures of rapid tempo, only to return to the original key of C. The student is advised to make similar alternative analyses in similar cases, weighing for himself their advantages and disadvantages as descriptions of the harmonic effect.

EX. 478. Weber—*Overture to "Der Freischütz"*

THE MODULATING SEQUENCE

The commonest form of modulating sequence embraces three keys. There is no return to the tonality of the initial pattern. The modulation does not take place within the pattern, but the final chord of the pattern is the pivot chord. The modulation to the second key is called a passing modulation since there is no permanence to the key. It represents a stage in the modulation to the third, or ultimate, key. Passing modulations are not necessarily sequential, but the modulating sequence does contain a passing modulation in its most common form.

EX. 479. Bach—*Well-tempered Clavier, I, Fugue no. 18*

In this example the modulation to E is a passing modulation. The suspension in the inside voice is helpful in avoiding the cadential effect at each final chord of the pattern. The first transposition moves down a major third and the second down a minor third, it being impossible to divide the interval of a perfect fifth (from the initial key, G-sharp, to the desired destination, C-sharp) into two equal parts. Moreover, there is a change of mode in the second key. The E minor triad is a poor chord in both the other keys, so E major is chosen.

The pattern used in a modulating sequence is usually constructed on a clearly tonal harmonic basis. This does not mean of necessity the inclusion of the tonic chord. In the example below the progression II–V serves very well to establish the tonal centers of three keys not closely related.

EX. 480. Brahms—*Symphony no. 2*

The modulating sequence has more possibilities as to the degree of transposition than the sequence with one tonal center. The following example shows a chromatic relationship between the keys.

EX. 481. Wagner—*Die Walküre, Act I*

KEYBOARD PRACTICE

The sequence is an extremely useful medium for the practice of harmonic progressions at the keyboard. The student should try to form sequences of all the harmonic formulae at his disposal, playing them throughout the length of the keyboard. His first problem will be to make a smooth connection between the pattern and its transposition. While there are some cases in which no really satisfactory connection can be made, it may be accepted as a principle that a solution always exists and is to be found by seeking. Weak progressions can be used if they are properly placed in the rhythmic scheme. Lengthening of the time values facilitates change of position of the voices. In the modulating sequence the last chord of the pattern is taken as pivot chord for the modulation.

It is strongly urged that the entire sequence be not written out. Two appearances of the pattern are enough to show the plan. The continuance of the sequence will then be a mental exercise rather than a mechanical reading or memorizing. As in all keyboard exercises, rhythmic playing (meaning rhythmic thinking) is essential, and a steady beat should be adhered to at all times, even though it must be very slow at first.

The literal extension of a nonmodulating sequential pattern throughout all its possible transpositions will often bring about one or two progressions which would not otherwise be employed, as for instance VII–IV, with its augmented fourth relationship. Such progressions are considered justified by the logic of the symmetrical melodic movement of the voices and need not be avoided in exercises.

The following are a few examples of beginnings of sequences, to be played the length of the keyboard, and in all keys.

THE SEQUENCE IN HARMONIZATION

A sequence in a melodic voice is not always accompanied by sequence in the other voices or in the harmony. It is nevertheless advisable in the study of harmony to treat sequences in given parts as harmonic sequences, until the facility is acquired of arranging these sequences whenever desired. Above all, the avoidance of sequential treatment should not be due to failure to notice the suggestion in the given part. Let it be understood as a convention that melodic sequences in the exercises of this book are to be treated as harmonic sequences.

EXERCISES

1. Work out the following figured basses:

2. Construct different sequences on the same harmonic background as those in Exs. 467, 468, 475, 479. Vary the tempo and the general melodic texture.

3. Construct phrases containing sequences fulfilling the following requirements:

a. A nonmodulating sequence in which the pattern contains three different chords and the transposition is upward by intervals of a third.

b. A modulating sequence in which the final chord of the pattern is VofV in the second key.

c. A modulating sequence which starts in the key of D and ends in the key of A-flat.

d. A nonmodulating sequence which employs secondary dominants in the form of diminished seventh chords.

4. Harmonize the following unfigured basses:

5. Harmonize the following melodies:

Twenty | NONDOMINANT HARMONY— SEVENTH CHORDS

Harmony of dominant effect and triads make up the bulk of the harmonic material in the common-practice period. Dissonant chords of nondominant character are found to be comparatively unusual, when the whole period is considered. During the early part of the period they appear fairly often as the result of contrapuntal writing but at no time can these chords be said to have been exploited until the end of the nineteenth century, with composers like Fauré, Debussy, and Ravel, composers whose works are not of the common-practice period in harmony.

Just what the elements of dominant harmony are, is difficult to say. Harmonic meaning is naturally a matter of usage and convention. A few external features of the dominant effect can be pointed out, such as the presence of the leading-tone a major third above the root, and the strengthening of this impression by the addition of a seventh, a diminished fifth above the leading-tone. The intervals between the chord factors are what determine the harmonic significance of the chord when no resolution is present to show its function in the tonality.

Employing only the tones of the major and minor scales, the following seventh chords are constructed on the scale degrees other than the dominant:

EX. 482. TABLE OF NONDOMINANT SEVENTH CHORDS

These chords are called secondary seventh chords by some theorists.

It will be observed that the chords marked *a* are derived from the major scale, those marked *b* from the minor scale in its harmonic form. Those marked *c* result from the use of the melodic minor scale and those marked *d* are chords containing the minor sixth degree and the major third degree. All these variants are made possible by the variations in the scale degrees and are not chromatically altered chords.

The nondominant character of these chords will be brought out by comparing each to a dominant chord built upon the same bass note, either a dominant seventh or an incomplete dominant ninth. To put the question another way, the student should ask himself what chromatic alterations would be necessary to change these chords into secondary dominants.

Such an examination will reveal that II_7b, IV_7c, VI_7c, and VII_7 are similar in interval construction to dominant forms. The true identity of these chords becomes clear only upon their resolution.

Five of the chords remaining may be grouped together as having the same kind of sonority due to their intervals, which are minor third, perfect fifth, and minor seventh. These are I_7c, II_7a, III_7a, IV_7b, VI_7a.

Four others comprise still another group, with the intervals major third, perfect fifth, and major seventh. The last-named interval imparts a sharpness and pungency to the dissonant sound of the chords of this group, I_7a, III_7c, IV_7a, VI_7b.

There remain two groupings of two chords each. I_7b and IV_7d are alike in their intervals, minor third, perfect fifth, and major seventh, and finally III_7b and VI_7d are similar, with major third, augmented fifth, and major seventh. The last two groups have in common the interval of the augmented fifth between two factors of the chord. This gives a certain marked harmonic color associated with these chords.

The ability to distinguish by sound the chords of the above groups should be acquired by practice. The chords should be played for ear-training in root position and in all inversions, with variations in spacing and range.

PREPARATION

The remarks made in Chapter Thirteen on the subject of the preparation of dissonance apply as well to the nondominant dissonances. It is our concern to derive principles regarding the common practice of composers in the use of harmonic material, and we cannot say that the principle of strict preparation of dissonances really exists in common harmonic practice. It is true that in certain styles of writing the nondominant seventh enters most often as a suspension or repeated tone, but this observation would hardly be applicable to the divergent styles of the eighteenth and nineteenth centuries.

THE NONHARMONIC ELEMENT

The question of deciding whether a tone is a chord factor or a nonharmonic tone comes often to the fore in the study of harmony. More important than the decision of this question is the appreciation of both sides of the issue. Let us repeat that all chords are the product of the momentary coincidence of melodic parts. A vertical cross-section of the music at a given instant is undeniably a chord, but we notice that some of these chords are constantly recurring under different conditions whereas others seem to depend on some other simpler chord for their existence.

The absurd extremes of theoretical explanation might be established as follows:

EX. 483

C: I^{13} I   I————

In the first case the A has been taken to be the top factor in a thirteenth chord of which the seventh, ninth, and eleventh are missing! In the second case the D, B, and F have been diagnosed as appoggiature on the tonic triad. Without denying the literal truth of these analyses, their palpable absurdity can likewise be admitted. Most cases will contain elements of both extremes.

Some of the nondominant seventh chords appear ordinarily in a form which does not necessitate analysis as a seventh chord, but their relative importance as harmonic effects should be taken into account.

RESOLUTION

The seventh of the chord resolves customarily by moving down one degree. Harmonically, the regular resolution is to the chord whose root is a perfect fourth higher, except in the case of IV$_7$ and the minor VI$_7$, where the perfect fourth above would lie outside the scale. The resolutions are shown below.

Irregular resolutions are also employed, although not as often in practice as the possibilities would lead one to expect.

The fifth, or the third, is sometimes omitted, especially when the resolution is made to another seventh chord. In such a case the root is doubled.

The inversions resolve contrapuntally in much the same way as the root position, except that the root will usually remain stationary rather than move up a fourth.

THE TONIC SEVENTH

EX. 484

$$\text{I}^7\ \text{IV} \quad \text{I}^7\ \text{IV} \quad \text{I} \quad \text{I}^2\ \text{II}^4_3 \quad \text{I}^4_3\ \text{IV} \quad \text{I}^6_5\ \text{IV} \quad \text{I} \quad \text{I}^7\ \text{IV}$$

Regular resolution to IV. In the minor mode the lowered seventh degree is used in order to descend melodically to the minor sixth degree.

EX. 485. Brahms—*Intermezzo, op. 117, no. 2*

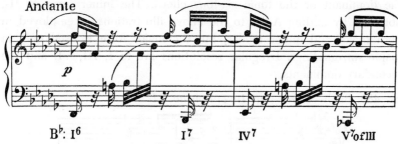

B♭: I⁶   I⁷   IV⁷   V⁷ofIII

The seventh occurs fairly often as appoggiatura to the octave of the root.

The commonest irregular resolution is to II₇, the root remaining in position to become the seventh of the second chord.

In the following example, too, the root remains static, making a six-four chord of the subdominant triad.

EX. 486. Grieg—*Sonata, op. 7*

C: IV⁶₄   I⁷   IV⁶₄   I

THE SUPERTONIC SEVENTH

EX. 487

II⁷ V   II⁷ V⁷   II⁶₅ V   II⁴₃ V   II² V⁶₅   II⁷ I⁶

II⁶₅ I⁶₄   II⁷ III   II⁷ VI

Regular resolution to V. This chord is common in cadences, before the dominant or the tonic six-four chord. The minor form of II$_7$, obtained by adding A-flat to the above illustrations, is employed in both major and minor modes, but the major form is used only in major surroundings. Irregular resolutions are to I, III, VI, and the secondary dominants.

EX. 488. Bach—*Three-part Invention no. 11*

B♭: VI   II$_5^6$ V^7

EX. 489. Schumann—*Symphony no. 1*

C: VI^6 II^7 V   I

EX. 490. Berlioz—*"Fantastic" Symphony*

C: IV   V of V   II$_5^6$ I

EX. 491. Brahms—*String Quartet, op. 51, no. 2*

A: IV   I^6 II^7(C♯ app.)   V$_2^o$ IV^6

THE MEDIANT SEVENTH

EX. 492

$$\text{III}^7 \quad \text{VI} \qquad \text{III}^6_5 \quad \text{VI} \qquad \text{III}^4_3 \quad \text{VI} \qquad \text{III}^7 \quad \text{VI} \qquad \text{III}^7 \quad \text{VI}$$

Regular resolution to VI. The two minor forms differ in the action of the fifth, which ascends when it is the leading-tone and descends when it is the lowered seventh degree. Irregular resolutions of III₇ are to IV, II, and the secondary dominants.

EX. 493. Chopin—*Etude, op. 10, no. 1*

$$\text{C:} \quad \text{III}^7 \qquad \text{VI}^7$$

EX. 494. Mattheson—*Gigue*

$$\text{D:} \quad \text{III}^7 \quad \text{VI}^7 \quad \text{II}^7 \quad \text{V}^7\text{of V} \quad \text{V} \quad \text{I}$$

THE SUBDOMINANT SEVENTH

EX. 495

$$\text{IV}^7 \, \text{II}^6_5 \quad \text{V} \qquad \text{IV}^7 \text{II}^6 \quad \text{V} \qquad \text{IV}^7 \, \text{II}^6_5 \quad \text{V} \qquad \text{IV}^7 \, \text{II}^6_5 \quad \text{V} \qquad \text{IV}^7 \text{V} \quad \text{IV}^7 \text{V}$$

The regular resolution of IV_7 is not to the root a fourth above, which would be VII. In the majority of cases the seventh moves down before the progression of the other tones of the chord, making a form of II_7, which then proceeds to V. The seventh is therefore usually considered an appoggiatura.

EX. 496. Bach—*Chorale: Herzliebster Jesu*

EX. 497. Beethoven—*String Quartet, op. 18, no. 1*

EX. 498. Bach—*Well-tempered Clavier, I, Prelude no. 1*

When the fifth is omitted the root will be doubled and the supertonic chord which usually follows will be a triad in first inversion.

EX. 499. Haydn—*String Quartet, op. 20, no. 4*

The direct resolution of IV$_7$ to V is less common and calls for care in the arrangement of the voices to avoid parallel fifths. Two such arrangements are shown in Ex. 495. In the following example the progression is made smoother by the use of a tonic six-four chord.

EX. 500. Brahms—*Sonata for Violin and Piano, op. 108*

Irregular resolutions are practicable to I and to several of the secondary dominants. The example below shows an unusual progression by parallel motion to III$_7$.

EX. 501. Bach—*Sonata no. 1 for Violin alone*

THE SUBMEDIANT SEVENTH

EX. 502

Regular resolution to II. When the third is present it will be prolonged or repeated, becoming the seventh of II.

EX. 503. Handel—*Suite no. 8*

As in the last of the progressions shown in Ex. 502, the voices may pass over a form of IV₇ before reaching the II chord, or the resolution may sound like both IV and II. The harmonic rhythm may be either weak-to-strong or strong-to-weak. In the latter case the seventh will sound as appoggiatura to its note of resolution.

EX. 504. Mendelssohn—*Symphony no. 3*

In the example below, the chord resolves irregularly to a sub-dominant chord with root chromatically raised.

EX. 505. Haydn—*String Quartet, op. 76, no. 2*

Although the form of VI₇ which combines the major sixth degree with the minor third degree ordinarily occurs when the sixth degree is part of an ascending melodic minor scale, it may also be found resulting from a descending chromatic movement.

EX. 506. Rameau—*La Livri*

THE LEADING-TONE SEVENTH

This chord, usually an incomplete dominant ninth, partakes of nondominant characteristics when it proceeds to III.

EX. 507. Bach—*French Suite no. 5: Gigue*

NONDOMINANT SEVENTHS IN SEQUENCE

The continuous series of seventh chords is a favorite device in non-modulating sequences. The sevenths usually enter as suspensions, and when the chords are in root position every other chord will be incomplete, with its root doubled.

EX. 508

All inversions may be employed in these sequences, as well as ornamental resolutions of the suspensions and other melodic devices.

EX. 509. Krebs—*Partita no. 6: Allemande*

$$B^\flat: \quad VI^7 \quad II^7 \quad V^7 \quad I^7 \quad IV^7 \; VII^7 \; III^7 \quad V\text{of}V \qquad V$$

MODULATION

The nondominant seventh chords are useful as pivot chords in modulation. Since they are not of dominant effect they do not strongly suggest the key, and for each of these chords there is at least one other of identical sound. For instance, the II_7 of C major may be interpreted also as I_7 of D minor, III_7 of B-flat major, IV_7 of A minor, or VI_7 of F major.

Irregular resolutions are sometimes useful in confirming the interpretation of the second key. For example, in a modulation from F to B-flat, if the pivot chord is VI_7 in F becoming III_7 in B-flat, the regular resolution will be heard as a chord still in F.

EX. 510

$$\begin{cases} F:VI^7 \quad B^\flat: VI \\ B^\flat: III^7 \; (F: II) \end{cases}$$

If, on the other hand, the irregular resolution III_7 to IV is employed in B-flat, it will be evident to the ear that a modulation has taken place, since the chord of resolution is not a usual chord in the key of F.

EX. 511

$$\begin{cases} F: VI^7 \quad B^\flat: IV \\ B^\flat: III^7 \end{cases}$$

FORMULAE

The numerous formulae for keyboard practice afforded by this group of chords are by no means exhausted by those given in Exs. 484, 487, 492, 495, 502, 508. The student is expected to add others, especially formulae using inversions and irregular resolutions, either originally constructed or gathered from musical literature.

EXERCISES

1. Work out the following figured basses:

2. Construct a phrase containing a sequence, the pattern of which has for its harmonic background the progression II_2–$III\,{}^4_3$.

3. Construct a musical sentence of three phrases, fulfilling the following specifications:

a. The first phrase modulates from D major to F-sharp minor by means of a nondominant seventh chord as pivot chord.

b. The second phrase contains a modulating sequence ending in some key other than D.

c. The third phrase returns to D major by a modulation using a nondominant seventh as pivot chord.

4. Harmonize the following unfigured basses, introducing nondominant seventh chords:

5. Harmonize the following melodies, introducing nondominant seventh chords:

Twenty-one | NINTH, ELEVENTH, AND THIRTEENTH CHORDS

It would seem a natural process in the evolution of harmonic usage to continue superposing intervals of a third in order to increase the vocabulary of chords. Conscious efforts to accomplish this, however, are not observed in the works of composers of the common-practice period in harmony. Furthermore, there is as yet no evidence to show that developments in this direction in the twentieth century have led to more than an occasional use of chords of the eleventh and thirteenth as pure chords.

One important influential factor in this result is the firm establishment of the principle of four-part writing as the norm of melodic texture. Despite the apparent complexity of much instrumental music it will usually lend itself to a reduction to not more than four real parts. Writing in less than four such parts is not at all uncommon, but it is rare that a composer employs more than four, or five at the most.

This fact is consistently demonstrated by harmonic analysis, the continued practice of which on the part of the student is here taken for granted. It is again recommended that in the written exercises there be no departure from the principle of the four-part harmonic background. The type of exercise described in Chapter Six should be used throughout the study of all the harmonic material.

When a chord of five factors, like the ninth chord, is rendered by four parts, one factor must be omitted unless one of the parts sounds two factors in turn. It has been seen that in the dominant ninth the ninth is often either a melodic or a harmonic tone, depending upon its prominence as a harmonic ingredient. Similar attributes have been noted in the nondominant seventh chords, especially IV. This ambiguity of function becomes even more marked in the non-dominant ninth chords, and the chords of the eleventh and thirteenth, so-called. The omission of factors weakens the sense of structure in thirds and allows the ear to accept the higher factors as melodic tones dependent on a simple harmonic background, usually a triad, or dominant seventh chord.

In the following example, a thirteenth chord is shown (*a*) with all its factors, a sonority quite foreign to the period of harmonic common practice. It is also shown (*b*) as it usually occurs. Playing of this second arrangement will demonstrate the high improbability of the missing thirds, especially A and C, and will also show the strong implication in the note E that it represents D, whether or not it actually resolves to it.

EX. 512

The nondominant ninth chord effects used by composers are generally found on the roots I, II, and IV, less often on III, or VI. They are brought about in nearly all cases by the presence of one or more appoggiature or suspensions.

THE APPOGGIATURA

The appoggiatura to the octave above the bass, if sufficiently prominent harmonically, will create the effect of a ninth chord. If the seventh is not present the true chord is a triad in root position.

EX. 513

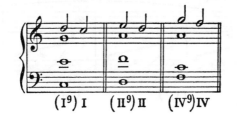

$(I^9)\ I \qquad (II^9)\ II \qquad (IV^9)\ IV$

When the seventh is included and both seventh and ninth resolve, as a double appoggiatura, the fundamental harmony is a chord of the sixth.

EX. 514

(I^9) VI^6 (II^9) VII^6 (IV^9) II^6

Both fifth and seventh may be included with the ninth, representing a seventh chord in first inversion.

EX. 515

(I^9) VI^6_5 (II^9) VII^6_5 (IV^9) II^6_5

All of the appoggiature shown may occur in the form of suspensions, in which case they would enter as tied-over notes from the preceding chord and would, of course, be weak instead of strong rhythmically.

These effects are also used in the minor mode, the lowered seventh degree being employed when it descends to the sixth.

III_9 and VI_9 have been omitted from the above examples as they are little used, but these effects may be seen in the following examples.

EX. 516. Brahms—*Ballade, op. 10, no. 4*

B: VI^6_5 (VI^9) $\mathrm{V}^7\text{of}\,\mathrm{V}$ V

In the example above, the ninth of the VI⁹ chord is a passing tone, rather than an appoggiatura. The following excerpt shows what might be called a III⁹ chord, created contrapuntally by two suspensions.

EX. 517. Bach—*Well-tempered Clavier, I, Prelude no. 7*

$$E\flat: VII^2 \quad III^6 \quad IV^6_5 \quad VII \quad (III^9) \quad I^6 \quad V \qquad I^7 \quad VI^6 \quad V^2 \text{of} VV^6$$

The ninths representing harmony of II or IV are the commonest of the nondominant ninths.

EX. 518. Beethoven—*Sonata for Violin and Piano, op. 30, no. 2*

$$A\flat: I \qquad (IV^9)II^6 \qquad II \qquad V$$

APPOGGIATURE WITH DELAYED RESOLUTION

Sometimes the appoggiatura, or suspension, is delayed in its resolution so that a change of harmony takes place before the melodic tone is resolved. The nondominant ninth seems under these circumstances to possess more independence as a chord, although its contrapuntal origin is still apparent.

EX. 519. Beethoven—*Symphony no. 2*

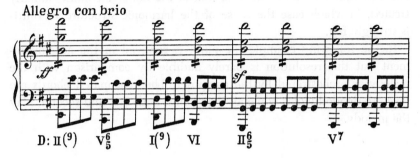

$$D: II(^9) \qquad V^6_5 \qquad I(^9) \qquad VI \qquad II^6_5 \qquad V^7$$

EX. 520. Schumann—*Symphony no. 3*

The following is an unusual example in that all factors of the ninth chord are sounded, so that the effect is that of a true supertonic ninth.

EX. 521. Grieg—*Sonata, op. 7*

THE UNRESOLVED APPOGGIATURA

As a final stage in the evolution of a chord the contrapuntal tone is left unresolved. It is nevertheless essential in the nondominant ninth chord, as well as in the chords of the eleventh and thirteenth, that the character of these higher factors, as contrapuntal tones whose resolution is not sounded but implied, be recognized. The effect is somewhat different from that of the dominant ninth similarly treated, in which case the sense of the harmonic structure in thirds is strongly felt.

In the following example the ninth is resolved in the accompaniment but this resolution is barely audible by comparison with the melody as orchestrated by the composer. The syncopated chords are given to divided violas while all the violins, both first and second, play the melody.

EX. 522. Schumann—*Symphony no. 2*

Eb: II9   V9   I9   I6   II6   VofV

The ninth in the example below cannot in any sense be said to resolve. Note also that the chord is in the first inversion. Inversions of these chords are not common, the interval of a ninth being ordinarily formed with the bass.

EX. 523. Franck—*Quintet*

F: V   I7/6/5   V4/3   I

Part of the charm of the cadence in the following example derives from the uncertainty as to the contrapuntal significance of the double appoggiatura, E, C-sharp. It is as though the seventh and ninth of the subdominant were held over from the tonic chord and the group of sixteenth-notes were decorated auxiliaries.

EX. 524. Mozart—*Pianoforte Concerto, K. 488*

A: I   V7ofIV   IV6/4   II6   V°6   I6   IV9   I

THE PEDAL

Consideration of chords of the eleventh and thirteenth brings up the subject of the pedal (pedal point, organ point), a technical device which often plays a large part in the making of these chords.

The name "pedal" is applied to a tone which persists in one voice throughout several changes of harmony. It tends to render the harmonic rhythm static and this effect is usually offset by the use of chords dissonant both in themselves and with the pedal. A good pedal will be at some moment foreign to the harmony with which it sounds, and it customarily begins and ends as a member of the harmony.

There are almost no restrictions as to the use of the pedal. It may appear as the bass, as the upper voice, or as an inner part. It may be any degree of the scale, although by far the commonest pedals are on the tonic and dominant, most often in the bass.

The term "pedal" originated as descriptive of the natural procedure of holding down an organ pedal while improvising above. As subsequently developed by composers, however, the device sometimes seems far from the implications of its name. It is often broken into rhythmic patterns and decorated by other tones, even attaining thematic significance in the ostinato figure.

The strength of tonality inherent in the pedal allows the accompanying harmony to go far afield without destroying the tonal unity of the music. A double pedal is sometimes used, tonic and dominant, making the key even more secure.

In more modern developments the pedal is considered one of the origins of polytonality. It is certain that when one key is represented by a pedal, perhaps a double or a triple pedal, one can easily hear a second key sounded simultaneously by harmony above.

THE CHORD OF THE ELEVENTH

The effects generally referred to as eleventh and thirteenth chords are brought about by the melodic means of the appoggiatura and the suspension, and also by the use of the pedal. The pedals usually employed are tonic and dominant.

The tonic eleventh effect may be created by a dominant seventh chord superimposed upon a tonic pedal.

EX. 525. Brahms—*Variations, op. 21, no. 1*

The same combination is very frequently arranged rhythmically so that the dominant chord is heard as an appoggiatura chord to the tonic, an effect conveniently described as "five over one."

EX. 526. Bach—*Partita no. 5: Preambulum*

EX. 527. Beethoven—*Sonata for Violin and Piano, op. 30, no. 1*

It may happen that the tonic part of the above sonority is represented by an actual chord or arpeggio while the dominant chord is still sounding. We then have all the factors of a tonic eleventh chord, but there can be no doubt that the upper three factors are heard as contrapuntal tones over a simple triad, rather than as chord members.

EX. 528. Beethoven—*Sonata, op. 2, no. 2*

A: V⁷   V/I (I¹¹) I

What is commonly referred to as the dominant eleventh is ordinarily the subdominant triad sounding over a dominant pedal.

EX. 529. Brahms—*Sonata, op. 5*

D♭:   I II IV(V₁₁) I II I   I
dom. ped.- - - - - - - - - - - - - - - - - - -

In the following example the dominant pedal lies both above and below the subdominant triad.

EX. 530. Brahms—*Intermezzo, op. 118, no. 2*

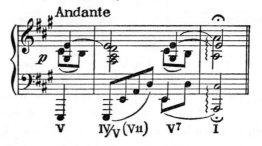

V   IV/V (V₁₁) V⁷   I

The eleventh may appear as a nonharmonic tone over the dominant ninth.

EX. 531. Beethoven—*Symphony no. 9*

Eleventh chord effects may be found on II and IV, resulting from appoggiature.

EX. 532. Mascagni—*Cavalleria Rusticana: Regina Coeli*

EX. 533. Liszt—*Sonata*

In the example below the interval of the eleventh is made by an appoggiatura with delayed resolution.

EX. 534. Rust—*Pianoforte Sonata no. 9*

Ninth and eleventh may both be present in the form of a double appoggiatura.

EX. 535. Beethoven—*Symphony no. 2*

EX. 536. Brahms—*Symphony no. 3*

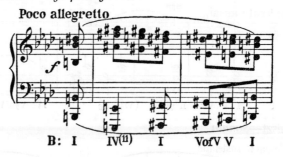

EX. 537. Mendelssohn—*String Quartet, op. 12*

THE CHORD OF THE THIRTEENTH

The thirteenth is as high as it is possible to go in the series of thirds, since the fifteenth would coincide with the double octave. The dominant thirteenth of contrapuntal origin is a fairly common chord effect. It has been pointed out that the third degree, that degree being the thirteenth above the dominant, tends to be absorbed into the dominant harmony when it stands above a dominant bass, as in III$_6$ and I$_4^6$. It is this third degree which gives rise to the expression "dominant thirteenth," especially when it occurs in combination with a dominant seventh chord (see Ex. 512).

In the following example the thirteenth appears as appoggiatura, really a sixth, to the fifth of the chord. The resolution is completed in the left-hand part.

EX. 538. Chopin—*Prelude, op. 45*

A: V^7(13)   VI

The same type of appoggiatura is shown below in its minor form, and over the dominant minor ninth. It is to be noted that in both of these chords the fifth is omitted until supplied by the resolution of the third degree.

EX. 539. Wagner—*Parsifal, Act I*

B: V^9(13)

The third degree may enter as échappée interpolated between the second degree and its destination, the tonic.

EX. 540

V^7(13)   I

Although not strictly speaking an échappée, the third degree in the example below is of similar effect. The D may also be explained as an anticipation.

EX. 541. Schumann—*Carnaval: Valse Noble*

The unresolved appoggiatura, often the means of suggesting the dominant thirteenth chord, is also clearly understood as a contrapuntal rather than a harmonic factor.

EX. 542. Brahms—*Intermezzo, op. 76, no. 4*

EX. 543. Chopin—*Polonaise-fantasie, op. 61*

If the following example contained a leading-tone in the first three measures the chord would sound as a real thirteenth. Without that factor the separation of subdominant harmony from the dominant bass is quite marked, so that a pedal effect is clearly present, continued from the preceding measures.

EX. 544. Dvořák—*Symphony no. 5*

G: IV⁷ II⁷ IV⁷ II⁷ IV⁷ II⁷   V⁷
dom.ped.------------------------------I

In the following unusual example the thirteenth is held through into the chord of resolution, as an unresolved contrapuntal tone. The chord does not, however, sound as a thirteenth chord. The other tones are those of the dominant seventh, leaving out the fifth, the implied resolution of the thirteenth.

EX. 545. Chopin—*Mazurka, op. 24, no. 4*

B♭: V⁷ (13)   I

So-called thirteenth chords may be found resulting from the placing of the dominant ninth over the tonic bass as a pedal.

EX. 546. Chopin—*Mazurka, op. 24, no. 1*

E♭: II   IV   I   V⁹(I¹³)
ton. ped.-----------------------------I

The dominant ninth used thus may be either major or minor and may occur without root.

272   *HARMONY*

EX. 547. Bach—*Well-tempered Clavier, II, Prelude no. 9*

The dominant ninth may appear as an appoggiatura chord over the tonic root, making a tonic thirteenth effect.

EX. 548. Mendelssohn—*Song without Words, op. 85, no. 5*

In the following example the complete tonic thirteenth is formed by a combination of the dominant ninth and the tonic triad. The dominant is represented by four suspensions which subsequently resolve into the tonic harmony.

EX. 549. Brahms—*Intermezzo, op. 119, no. 1*

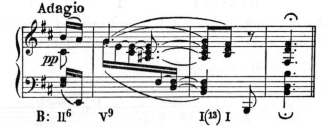

Formulae, to be played in all keys:

EXERCISES

1. Work out the following figured basses:

2. Construct original examples of the following harmonic effects, showing their introduction and resolution:

a. II_9 in G major, without seventh

b. IV_9 in E-flat minor, with fifth and seventh

c. I_9 in A major, resulting from an appoggiatura with delayed resolution

d. IV_9 in F minor, the ninth an unresolved appoggiatura

e. An inner dominant pedal

f. A tonic eleventh chord

g. A subdominant eleventh chord made by a double appoggiatura

h. A dominant thirteenth chord in which the thirteenth is an unresolved appoggiatura

3. Harmonize the following unfigured basses, using some chords of the ninth, eleventh, and thirteenth:

4. Harmonize the following melodies, introducing effects of chords of the ninth, eleventh, and thirteenth:

Twenty-two | THE RAISED SUPERTONIC AND SUBMEDIANT

IN a literal sense an altered chord is any chord affected by an accidental, signifying that one of its tones is changed from its original form as established by the key signature. There are three sources of these accidentals or chromatic alterations.

The first reason for the use of an accidental may be said to arise from the deficiency of our system of key signatures, inasmuch as the signatures do not permit the interchangeability of the modes as practiced by composers. Hence it is hardly necessary to speak of a chromatic alteration when a sharp, flat, or natural is used to indicate a normal scale degree. For example, we shall not apply the term "altered chords" to the following:

EX. 550

C: IV   III   II⁷   VI⁷

In the second category of chords affected by accidental signs are all the secondary dominants. These chords are not really altered chords. The process of deriving a secondary dominant chord is not that of altering a chord in the scale of the main key, but rather of adopting a temporary tonality in which the secondary dominant exists as a normal, unaltered chord. Some theorists use the expression "borrowed chords" for the secondary dominants. This category accounts for the greater part of the accidentals seen in music, except perhaps for actual modulations when the key signature has not been changed.

Keeping to the vocabulary of chords in the common practice of composers, there remains the group of chords which have chromatic signs not derived from the above sources. The important members of this group are the raised supertonic and the raised submediant, the Neapolitan sixth, the chords of the augmented sixth, and the chords with altered fifth.

II♯ AND VI♯ RAISED

The seventh chords on supertonic and submediant, derived from the major mode, and having root and third chromatically raised, are non-dominant diminished seventh chords. It was pointed out in Chapter Sixteen that the identity of a diminished seventh chord is determined by its resolution. These two chords resolve to I and V_7 respectively.

EX. 551

The resolutions are typical of the principle that a chromatically altered tone receives a tendency to continue movement in the direction of its alteration. Both chords contain raised tones whose tendency is upward. They are like leading-tones or appoggiature. The root being thus altered does not seem like a harmonic root, but more like a melodic tendency tone. Sometimes these are called appoggiatura-chords, but this name is not always accurate since the harmonic rhythm of the resolution is often weak-to-strong.

NOTATION

Composers have shown indifference to the grammatical notation of these diminished seventh chords, not only in writing for keyboard instruments but also in music for strings or wind instruments. The raised second degree is often written as minor third degree and the raised sixth as lowered seventh degree.

EX. 552

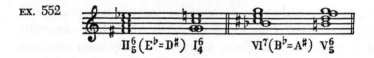

As written, VofV appears in place of II₇ and VofII for VI₇. The resolutions show both to be incorrect.

EX. 553. Bach—*Well-tempered Clavier, I, Prelude no. 3*

EX. 554. Beethoven—*Symphony no. 2*

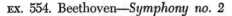

Music is fortunately a matter of sound rather than symbols, and there is no doubt that the second violins in the Beethoven example instinctively give the G-natural its proper meaning, that of an F-double-sharp.

The problem is more difficult in the example below.

EX. 555. Schubert—*Quintet, op. 163*

Here the viola part is obviously incorrectly written E-flat, for
D-sharp. But the melodic outline of the first violin part would be
strange, indeed, if D-sharp were substituted for E-flat. A compromise must be effected in performance between the harmonic and
the contrapuntal, a compromise that is continually necessary in music
of chromatic style and especially where enharmonic changes operate.

RHYTHM

When the chord and its resolution are in the rhythmic relation of
strong-to-weak, the chord has the character of an appoggiatura chord,
or three appoggiature over a single harmonic root.

EX. 556. Tchaikowsky—*Nutcracker Suite: Valse*

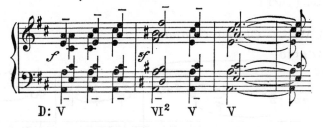

EX. 557. Chopin—*Impromptu, op. 36*

EX. 558. Brahms—*String Quintet, op. 111*

The voices may move as auxiliary tones, making an auxiliary chord of weak rhythmic value.

EX. 559. Rossini—*William Tell: Overture*

When the altered tones enter as chromatic passing tones the chord is a passing chord.

EX. 560. Weber—*Oberon: Overture*

EX. 561. Chopin—*Valse brillante, op. 34, no. 1*

These chords may also serve as independent chords of equal rhythmic value with the surrounding harmony. VI₇ is a useful chord for introducing the dominant half cadence to emphasize the key, and II₇ often appears prominently before the cadential six-four chord.

Ex. 562. Brahms—*Intermezzo, op. 119, no. 3*

Ex. 563. Mozart—*Concerto for Two Pianofortes, K. 365*

Ex. 564. Beethoven—*Sonata, op. 10, no. 2*

CROSS-RELATION

The two altered tones of either chord are sometimes found in a melodic group of double thirds or sixths forming a double cambiata. In this case the resulting cross-relations are not avoided. The altered tones may be first or second in the group.

Ex. 565

The above progressions contain not only the cross-relation, but also the unusual melodic interval of the diminished third, F to D-sharp and C to A-sharp. In the example below there are two cross-relations, A-flat to A-natural and F-natural to F-sharp. The melodic diminished third, A-flat to F-sharp, is accompanied in the top voice by the interval of a diminished fourth, D-flat to A-natural. It is the cambiata-like quality of the altered tones that makes this acceptable.

Ex. 566. Wagner—*Der Meistersinger, Act II*

MODE

The raised supertonic and submediant chords are more suggestive of the major mode than of the minor. VI_7 contains the major third degree and II_7 implies it by the raised second degree. Both chords may, however, be employed in the minor mode. If the resolution of II_7 is treated not as tonic, but as VofIV, there is no difficulty in continuing in minor. The following example shows VI_7 used in surroundings predominantly minor.

Ex. 567. Haydn—*String Quartet, op. 76, no. 4*

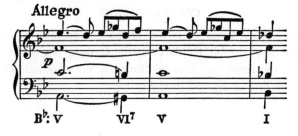

IRREGULAR RESOLUTION

Irregular resolution of diminished seventh chords in the harmonic sense of progression to an irregular root is rare. One such resolution is shown in Chapter Sixteen. Variations in the form of the chord of resolution can be employed, however, without destroying the identity of the diminished seventh.

In the resolution of II₇ raised, VofIV may be used, either as a dominant seventh chord or as an incomplete ninth, usually minor. The second case results in diminished seventh chords moving parallel.

EX. 568

The submediant chord may also resolve to an incomplete ninth.

EX. 569. Beethoven—*Symphony no. 3*

Allegro vivace

EX. 570. Bach—*Well-tempered Clavier, I, Prelude no. 8*

This resolution furnishes a key to the most convenient explanation of a series of consecutive diminished seventh chords moving chromatically upwards. Each pair of chords may be considered as the progression VI₇–V⁰₉.

EX. 571. Liszt—*Les Préludes*

Allegro

MODULATION

The use of the diminished seventh chord in a nondominant function adds greatly to the already numerous resources of that chord as a pivot chord in modulation. The modulation in which a dominant becomes a nondominant is especially effective and somewhat unexpected. For instance, if the incomplete dominant minor ninth of C is left as II_7 raised, the new key will be A-flat major. If it is left as VI_7 the distant key of D-flat will be introduced.

EX. 572

If it is desired that the pivot chord be VI_7 or II_7 in the first key, there are two problems. Since the identity of these chords depends upon their resolution, it is necessary that their function in the first key be made clear before the point of modulation. The best method of securing this clarity is to present the chord with its resolution in the first key, using it as a pivot chord only after its identity has been thus established to the hearer. The second problem is to avoid weakening the modulation by allowing the pivot chord to be the dominant of the second key. This can be arranged by using a secondary dominant.

Both of these procedures are seen in the following example:

EX. 573. Beethoven—*Symphony no. 7*

The pivot may be a nondominant diminished seventh chord in both keys. In the following example analysis reveals it to be based on the same degree in both tonalities, but with enharmonic change.

EX. 574. Franck—*String Quartet*

Formulae, to be played in all keys:

EXERCISES

1. Work out the following figured basses:

2. Construct a musical sentence of three phrases according to the following specifications:

a. The first phrase shows a diminished seventh chord used first as VofV, then as II₇ altered (with enharmonic change).

b. The second phrase modulates by means of a pivot chord which becomes VI₇ altered in the second key.

c. The third phrase returns to the original key by a pivot chord which is II₇ altered in the final key.

3. Construct a modulating sequence, the pattern of which contains the chord VI₇ altered.

4. Harmonize the following unfigured basses, introducing chords of the raised supertonic and submediant:

5. Harmonize the following melodies, introducing chords of the raised supertonic and submediant:

THE NEAPOLITAN SIXTH AND SUBDIVISIONS   287

5. Harmonize the following, using either introductory chords, altered subdominant, and submediant.

Twenty-three | THE NEAPOLITAN SIXTH

THE major triad having for its root the chromatically lowered second degree of the scale is known everywhere as the Neapolitan sixth. It is difficult to say wherein this chord is "Neapolitan," but the fact is that the name is of universal acceptance. In the earlier part of the period it was usually found in first inversion, hence the term "sixth." Later, however, the term "Neapolitan sixth" was applied to any arrangement of the triad, even root position.

Far from wishing to discard a definition so securely established by usage, we shall welcome the convenience of the identifying label attached to this chord. In this way we may be permitted the unscientific but quite understandable expression, "the Neapolitan sixth in root position," and the occasional use of the commonly accepted symbol N_6.

The Neapolitan sixth is a major triad and is, therefore, not a dissonant chord. However, the chromatic alteration of the second degree gives that tone a downward tendency so that when it proceeds upward there is a feeling of irregularity of movement, if not of irregular resolution.

Although derived from the minor scale, the Neapolitan sixth is freely used in either major or minor mode. It is a chord of strongly subdominant character, progressing most frequently to some form of the dominant chord.

288

EX. 575

Note that the bass is the best tone to double, as it is a tonal degree. The altered second degree is normally not doubled in the first inversion, but this is a rule less strictly followed in the case of the Neapolitan sixth than with any other chromatically altered chord.

The progressions shown in the example contain the cross-relation between D-flat and D-natural. It cannot be said that this cross-relation is avoided by composers, although there are many arrangements of the progression to V without it, as will be shown. The cross-relation may be seen in Exs. 577, 579, 581, and others.

When the dominant chord contains a seventh, its fifth will very likely be omitted so that no cross-relation will occur.

EX. 576. Beethoven—*Sonata, op. 27, no. 2*

The bass may remain in place as the harmony changes, making the third inversion of V₇.

EX. 577. Bach—*Suite for Flute and Strings*

If the sixth degree, fifth of the chord, is continued into the next harmony, a ninth chord will result.

EX. 578. Beethoven—*Sonata, op. 90*

The dominant ninth chord may be in its incomplete form, without root, most often as a diminished seventh chord. Unless the lowered second degree progresses upward, contrary to its tendency, the cross-relation will occur in this case.

EX. 579. Mozart—*String Quartet, K. 421*

Very often the dominant chord will first be represented by the cadential tonic six-four chord, the sixth and fourth as double appoggiatura. This allows a smooth stepwise progression in all voices, the three upper parts moving in contrary motion to the bass. The root succession is, of course, still II to V. The cross-relation is not noticeable because of the intervening harmonic effect of I.

EX. 580. Mozart—*Pianoforte Concerto, K. 488*

Other chords are sometimes interpolated between the Neapolitan sixth and the dominant. These are for the most part different forms of supertonic harmony. The problems of voice leading vary with the form chosen. If the chord is dominant of the dominant, there will be several chromatic progressions in the voices. Note, in the example below, that the cross-relation between the two forms of the second degree is permitted so that the lowered tone G-natural may descend according to its tendency. The other two chromatic progressions are effected each in a single voice.

EX. 581. Schumann—*String Quartet, op. 41, no. 3*

These problems of voice leading are sometimes obscured by the texture of instrumental writing, especially in music for keyboard instruments. In the following the altered second degree appears to be doubled and it is questionable whether the ear will follow the upward or the downward progression of that tone.

EX. 582. Mozart—*Fantasia, K. 397*

The following excerpt is clearer, as to the melodic progression of the parts, and it is evident that the lowered second degree moves upward. Doubling of the tone A, the sixth degree, avoids the cross-relation by allowing the progression A to A-sharp to be made in one voice.

In the first measure it is to be remarked that the melodic figuration over the Neapolitan sixth harmony takes the form of the scale of the temporary tonality of the lowered second degree, here D major.

EX. 583. Beethoven—*Sonata, op. 27, no. 2*

The altered tone may appear as appoggiatura to the tone below. The fundamental harmony will then be subdominant, although the peculiar color of the Neapolitan sixth should be recognized harmonically. It is also reasonable to consider the tonic as a passing tone, as in the following example:

EX. 584. Mozart—*Quintet, K. 515*

The above example shows the adaptability and coloristic effect of this chord employed in a passage which is prevailingly in the major mode.

The harmonic rhythm of the following cadential passage gives unusual prominence to the Neapolitan six-four.

EX. 585. Weber—*Overture to "Der Freischütz"*

The use of the Neapolitan sixth is not limited to cadential formulae. It may be found in any part of the phrase, and may even begin the piece.

EX. 586. Chopin—*Ballade, op. 23*

In its subdominant capacity it progresses occasionally to I or VofIV.

EX. 587. Handel—*Concerto Grosso no. 5*

EX. 588. Beethoven—*Trio, op. 1, no. 3*

The Neapolitan sixth may be used as subdominant harmony in a plagal cadence, followed by either major or minor tonic harmony.

EX. 589. Brahms—*String Quartet, op. 58, no. 1*

Another example by Brahms shows the chord in combination with the tonic note, making a seventh chord.

EX. 590. Brahms—*Symphony no. 4*

In the nineteenth century the Neapolitan sixth chord was employed with increasing frequency as a triad in root position. This gave the chord much more independence and stability, the lowered second degree being treated in this case not as a melodic tendency tone, but as a true harmonic root and so doubled. The doubled root and the augmented fourth relationship to the dominant help to emphasize the remoteness of this harmony from the main tonal center.

EX. 591. Chopin—*Prelude, op. 28, no. 20*

EX. 592. Brahms—*Sonata for Violin and Piano, op. 108*

D: VofIV   IV   II   I$^6_4$ V

Examples of the Neapolitan sixth in the six-four position are not numerous and usually such combinations are due to the presence of the lowered second degree as an appoggiatura (see Ex. 584).

The Neapolitan sixth may be preceded by its dominant, thus adding another to the list of secondary dominants available in one tonality.

EX. 593. Mozart—*Quintet, K. 581*

A: II^{6b} V^{2}ofN^6 II^{6b} I$^6_4$ V^7 I

EX. 594. Schubert—*Symphony no. 7*

A: V^{2}ofN^6 II^{6b} V^2 I^6 II^{6b} I$^6_4$ V

The independence of the root position chord is greatly strengthened by the presence of the secondary dominant "VofN$_6$." It is plain, however, that the two chords constitute an extension of the bounds of the main tonality rather than a weakening of it.

EX. 595. Chopin—*Mazurka, op. 7, no. 2*

FALSE MODULATION

It may happen that the tonality is actually so weakened by harmonies strongly suggestive of another tonal center that a modulation is felt to be the true effect, although there is an immediate return to the main tonality. In this case the term "false modulation" may be applied. The false modulation differs from the passing modulation by returning to the original key instead of proceeding to a third key.

In one sense the interpretation of a passage in analysis as false modulation may be considered as unnecessarily involving a change of key, since the relationship of any chord to a given tonality can be described in some way. But the general effect on the hearer should be taken into account, as well as the complexity of style of the music.

The Neapolitan sixth chord is often felt to be of sufficient tonal strength to cause a momentary shift to its root as a tonal center. This may be due simply to the length of time it occupies.

EX. 596. Chopin—*Prelude, op. 28, no. 6*

Or it may be because of the attendant harmonies. In the following example the last chord in the first measure is the raised supertonic in the key of G, followed by the tonic six-four. The use of the subdominant of G confirms this impression, but we know that the G-natural triad is but the Neapolitan sixth chord of the key of F-sharp.

EX. 597. Beethoven—*Sonata, op. 106*

MODULATION

The Neapolitan sixth is a useful pivot chord in modulation. As a simple major triad it is capable of many interpretations. It is common ground between distantly related keys, as in the following modulation from F to E.

EX. 598. Beethoven—*Sonata, op. 14, no. 1*

Formulae, to be played in all keys:

II$^{6b}_{3b}$ IV   V   II$^{6b}_{3b}$ V$^{o}_{9}$ofV   V   II$^{6b}_{3b}$ II$^{6}_{5}$ I$^{6}_{4}$ V VofN^{6} II V   I

EXERCISES

1. Work out the following figured basses:

2. Construct a modulating sequence in which the pivot chord is the Neapolitan sixth in the second key.

3. Explain the relationship of the Neapolitan sixth chord of the key of G to the tonalities A, F, E, F-sharp, and B-flat.

4. Show the progression of the Neapolitan sixth to five different chords in the key of D-flat.

5. Harmonize the following unfigured basses, introducing Neapolitan sixth chords:

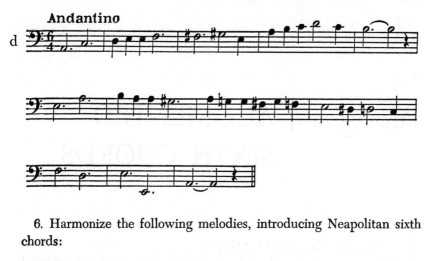

6. Harmonize the following melodies, introducing Neapolitan sixth chords:

Twenty-four | AUGMENTED SIXTH CHORDS

T HE four chords comprising the group known as augmented sixth chords have in common the interval of the augmented sixth created by the minor sixth degree and the chromatically raised fourth degree. The name "augmented sixth chord" derives from the commonest arrangement of the chords, in which this characteristic interval is found between the bass and an upper voice; but, as in the case of the Neapolitan sixth, it is often applied to other positions.

The augmented sixth chords are nondominant in function. They are strongly tonal since they indicate unmistakably the dominant of the key. The interval of the augmented sixth expands in its normal resolution to an octave which is the octave on the dominant.

EX. 599

This principle of tonality inherent in the augmented sixth chords is most important to an understanding of their use by composers of the common-practice period. Only by very uncommon exception is the octave of resolution anything other than dominant. The augmented sixth interval does not come from a dominant with lowered fifth, but from a subdominant with raised root. The following example shows its contrapuntal origin.

EX. 600

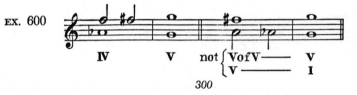

IV   V   not ⎰ V of V ——— V
                   ⎱ V ——————— I

The normal position of all four augmented sixth chords is that with the minor sixth degree in the bass and the raised fourth degree in any upper voice. Another voice is always the tonic, making three voices common to all four chords. Each member of the group will then be distinguished by the fourth voice.

EX. 601

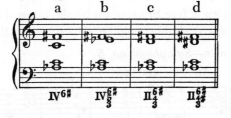

a is called the augmented sixth.

b is called the augmented six-five-three.

c is called the augmented six-four-three.

d is called the doubly augmented fourth.

Many theorists have used the names Italian sixth (*a*), German sixth (*b*), and French sixth (*c*). These names are not universally employed and have nothing like the established usage of the name Neapolitan sixth, for instance.

Note that *b* is like *a* with the minor seventh added; *d* sounds like *b*, but the difference between E-flat and D-sharp becomes clear on the resolution of the chord; *c* is distinguished from *b* by the presence of the second degree in place of the minor third degree; *a*, *b*, and *d* sound like dominant sevenths.

RESOLUTION

The regular resolution of the augmented sixth chords is to V, or V preceded by I$_4^6$. The raised fourth degree moves up a half step, the minor sixth degree moves down a half step, and the tonic either moves down directly to the leading-tone or remains in place as a suspension or appoggiatura before descending.

The fourth voice will, of course, vary in movement according to its identity. In *a*, the plain augmented sixth chord, since there are but three factors the tonic will be doubled. It is not customary to double either of the tones making the interval of the augmented sixth. The fourth voice usually moves up by step.

EX. 602

The fourth voice is free to move up by the interval of a fifth to the dominant, often a desirable melodic skip when in the upper voice.

EX. 603. Beethoven—*Symphony no. 5*

In the augmented six-five-three (*b*) the fourth voice forms with the bass an interval of a perfect fifth. The parallel fifths arising from the natural progression to the dominant are practiced except when occurring between soprano and bass. They are most often seen between tenor and bass. The third degree is, however, more frequently tied over as a suspension, or repeated as an appoggiatura, before continuing down to the second degree.

The augmented six-five-three is strongly indicative of the minor mode, since it contains both minor third and minor sixth degrees.

EX. 604

EX. 605. Mozart—*Sonata, K. 332*

The parallel fifths are more noticeable in the following example.

EX. 606. Franck—*Symphony*

This form of subdominant harmony is very common preceding the cadential six-four chord. Its tonal clarity is especially useful after a modulation.

EX. 607. Mozart—*Overture to "Don Giovanni"*

EX. 608. Brahms—*Intermezzo, op. 117, no. 2*

The augmented six-four-three (*c*) is built on the root II, instead of IV as with the two chords just described. It should be regarded nevertheless as a chord of subdominant function. The same chord may be reached by the process of lowering the fifth of a dominant seventh chord, in this case VofV, but this is a more advanced and much less common form of chromatic alteration and it implies a different tonal function.

The presence of the second degree affords a common tone between the augmented six-four-three and the dominant chord, so this factor will usually be repeated or tied over in this chord of resolution, although it may progress to an appoggiatura of the second degree.

EX. 609

EX. 610. Schubert—*String Quartet, op. 125, no. 1*

The augmented six-four-three is employed in connection with chords characteristic of the major mode as well as those of the minor, contributing to the impression of interchangeability of the two modes.

EX. 611. Chopin—*Nocturne, op. 48, no. 2*

In the chord of the doubly augmented fourth (*d*) the distinguishing factor is the raised second degree, implying a resolution to the major third degree. This interval of the doubly augmented fourth, formed between the minor sixth degree bass and the raised second degree, is harmonically identical with the perfect fifth. The chord can be told from the augmented six-five-three only upon its resolution.

EX. 612

EX. 613. Chopin—*Ballade, op. 47*

Composers frequently write the doubly augmented fourth incorrectly as an augmented six-five-three. It will be recalled that the same indifference as to the notation of the raised second degree was observed in the supertonic seventh chord with raised root and third. The two chords are closely related, differing only in the form of the sixth degree.

EX. 614. Haydn—*String Quartet, op. 64, no. 5*

When the augmented sixth is followed by a dominant seventh chord, the raised fourth degree descends chromatically, somewhat in the manner of the irregular resolution of a leading-tone. If the augmented six-five-three is used, the progression sounds like a succession of dominant seventh chords and is often so written, though incorrectly.

The steps in the evolution of this progression might be outlined as follows:

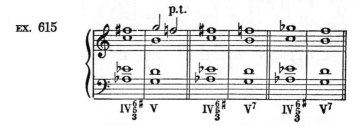

EX. 615

In the following example, the parallel motion is interrupted by the appoggiatura in the upper voice:

EX. 616. Beethoven—*Sonata, op. 57*

Coloristic possibilities of the augmented sixth combined with chromatic nonharmonic tones are suggested in the following well-known quotation.

EX. 617. Wagner—*Prelude to "Tristan and Isolde"*

The appoggiatura forming the interval of a diminished octave with the raised fourth degree is of fairly frequent occurrence.

EX. 618. Mozart—*Sonata, K. 576*

F#: I   VI⁷   IV⁶₅#   V

INVERSIONS

Dispositions of the factors of these chords with other than the sixth degree in the bass does not seem to destroy their identity as chords of the augmented sixth, even though the characteristic interval is found between less prominent voices, or inverted to become a diminished third. This accounts for such expressions as "the augmented six-five-three in the six-four-three position," meaning that the chord normally found making the intervals six, five, and three has been rearranged so that it makes the intervals six, four, and three.

It is recommended that the augmented sixth chords be regarded simply as forms of II and IV with alterations as shown above, using the Arabic numerals to designate in the customary way the intervals formed with the bass.

When the raised fourth degree is in the bass the resultant interval of a diminished third resolves with no less emphasis to the octave of the dominant.

EX. 619. Brahms—*Waltz, op. 39, no. 7*

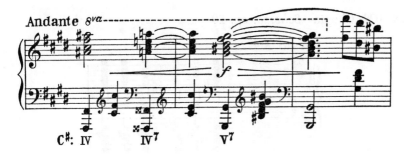

C#: IV   IV⁷   V⁷

EX. 620. Bach—*B-minor Mass: Crucifixus*

(voice parts only)

In the above examples, the position of the chord is a natural consequence of the melodic progression of the two outside voices in contrary motion chromatically. The melodic movement of the bass is usually the reason for a choice of some factor other than the sixth degree as a bass note.

A static bass on the tonic or third degree may hold through an augmented sixth appearing above as double auxiliary or double appoggiatura.

EX. 621. Brahms—*Violin Concerto, op. 77*

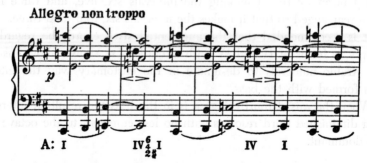

As a dissonant chord over a dominant pedal the augmented sixth is strikingly effective.

EX. 622. Chopin—*Scherzo, op. 20*

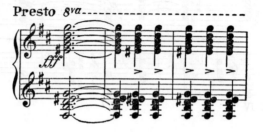

IRREGULAR RESOLUTION

Harmonically, the augmented sixth chords have few irregular resolutions. These are mostly progressions to tonic harmony, as in Ex. 621. With the sixth degree in the bass, the progression to I in root position, the augmented sixth interval resolving in a direct fifth, was rarely used until late in the period, when it is recognized as a characteristic feature of the harmonic style of César Franck.

EX. 623. Franck—*Sonata for Violin and Piano*

Many irregularities in voice leading are possible in the regular root progression to V, because of the variety of forms of dominant harmony and the added resources of nonharmonic tones (see Ex. 617). In the following example the doubly augmented fourth leads to an effect of dominant thirteenth.

EX. 624. Schumann—*Symphonic Studies, op. 13*

MODULATION

As a pivot chord in modulation the augmented sixth is most often employed for the advantage of its enharmonic similarity to a dominant seventh chord. The raised fourth degree then becomes the seventh of the chord, a tone of downward tendency. Since the minor sixth degree is interpreted as a dominant the two tonalities involved will be a half-tone apart.

EX. 625. Beethoven—*String Quartet, op. 59, no. 3*

The above modulation is of the sudden type, since the pivot chord is the dominant of the new key. Somewhat different is the effect of the opposite arrangement, where the pivot chord is the augmented sixth chord in the second key. Both modulations may be described as unusual, however, in that the changes are to distantly related tonalities.

EX. 626. Schubert—*Symphony no. 8*

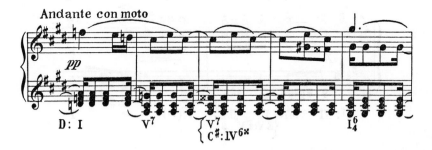

Owing to the tonal strength of the augmented sixth chord, it is often best to analyze it as being in the second key of the modulation, with the pivot chord coming before it.

EX. 627. Wagner—*Die Walküre: Act 2, Scene 4*

$$F\sharp : I \quad IV^{6\sharp} \quad I^{6}_{4} \quad IV^{7} \quad \begin{cases} F\sharp : II^{7} \\ B : VI^{7} \end{cases} \quad II^{6\sharp}_{3} \quad V^{7}$$

EXCEPTIONAL FORMS

A few cases may be found of chords having the same interval structure as chords of the augmented sixth group but derived from other degrees of the scale. One of these has been mentioned—that formed by the lowered second degree in a dominant seventh chord. Although properly considered a chord with altered fifth, it may be cited here as an instance of the comparatively rare treatment of the augmented sixth as a dominant.

EX. 628. Schubert—*Quintet, op. 163*

$$C : I \qquad V^{4}_{3} \qquad I$$

The supertonic seventh chord with major sixth degree and raised root is sometimes used in progression to I. It is similar in sound to the augmented six-five-three in the relative minor.

EX. 629. Grieg—*Song, "Hoffnung"*

$$E\flat : II^{6\sharp}_{5} \qquad I$$

FORMULAE

In addition to the four-part formulae given in Exs. 602, 604, 609, and 612, the following sequences are recommended for keyboard practice. They should not be written out, but played from the patterns given.

EXERCISES

1. Work out the following figured basses:

2. Write a modulating sequence in which the pivot chord is V₇ofIV becoming the chord of the doubly augmented fourth in the second key.

3. Construct a musical sentence of two phrases according to the following specifications:

   a. The first phrase modulates from B to B-flat by means of a pivot chord which is an augmented sixth in the second key.

   b. The second phrase returns to B by means of a passing modulation through a third key.

4. Harmonize the following unfigured basses, introducing augmented sixth chords:

5. Harmonize the following melodies, introducing augmented sixth chords:

Twenty-five | OTHER CHROMATIC CHORDS

THERE remain but few altered chords that we can include in the vocabulary of harmonic material in the common practice of composers. It is physically possible through the process of chromatic alteration to create a large number of new forms, just as one can spell new words with the letters of a language; but our purpose in this study is to define the harmonic vocabulary as employed.

Much can be learned about this common practice by experimenting with the possible alterations of existing chords with a view to discovering reasons why some forms were used in preference to others. The student should go about this systematically, taking each chord in turn and applying to it various chromatic alterations of the factors, appraising the results for the combination of intervals obtained and the relation of the chord to the tonality.

It will be observed immediately that a large proportion of the chords made by this method are really heard enharmonically as other more familiar chords, so that the apparent new form exists only on paper. A few such results are given here:

EX. 630

315

The harmonic interpretation of these forms depends upon the acceptance by the ear of the tones as particular scale degrees of a particular key and mode. In the above example the key of C is arbitrarily chosen but, as we know, it can be established aurally only through association with other harmonic elements. So the context will influence strongly the interpretation of chromatic tones. The following example contains a chromatic passing tone creating the augmented triad on C. If, however, the third of the chord is minor, the passing tone will be heard as the minor sixth degree instead of the raised fifth, and the progression is diatonic rather than chromatic.

EX. 631

C: I ——— VI   I   VI ———

The following observations are made as to chromatic alteration of the scale degrees:

The tonic may be raised, but if lowered it is heard as seventh degree.

The supertonic may be either raised or lowered. When raised it is sometimes heard as minor third degree.

The minor mediant if raised becomes the major mediant; if lowered it is heard as supertonic.

The major mediant if raised is heard as subdominant; if lowered it becomes minor third degree.

The subdominant may be raised, but if lowered it is heard as third degree.

The dominant may be raised, sometimes being heard thus as minor sixth degree. When lowered it will usually be heard as leading-tone of the dominant.

The minor submediant when raised becomes the major submediant; if lowered it is heard as dominant.

The major submediant may be raised, sometimes being heard thus as lowered seventh degree. When lowered it becomes minor sixth degree.

The leading-tone if raised is heard as tonic. It may be lowered.

New chords are the result of harmonic and melodic, vertical and horizontal, influences. Harmonically, they arise from a desire to add to the harmonic interest and variety by the creation of a sonority hitherto unheard, or by the use of an established form in an unaccustomed position in the tonality. Melodically, the altered tones forming the new chord are introduced for their value as tendency tones imparting melodic direction and continuity.

These two aspects are not entirely separate. Some of the altered chords appear most often as the effect of chromatic passing tones or other melodic tones. Some, like the raised supertonic, are almost entirely made up of tones capable of analysis as nonharmonic factors. Those vertical combinations which by their recurrence in music seem to have been brought about deliberately should be recognized as chords, albeit with certain qualifications. It will be recalled that this point of view had to be taken in the case of the six-four chord, the ninth, eleventh, and thirteenth chords, and even some seventh chords.

The appearance of chromatic tones has been studied thus far in these harmonic groups: the secondary dominants; the altered chords II_7 VI_7, the Neapolitan sixth, and the augmented sixth group. Other resources of chromatic alteration remain to be described.

THE AUGMENTED FIFTH

Chords with fifth raised to make the interval of the augmented fifth above the root are found on I, IV, and V.

The tonic chord so altered is practically always the major form. The altered tone is of course not doubled and the chord resolves regularly to the subdominant.

EX. 632

It also leads smoothly into the supertonic seventh chord, especially when the third degree is doubled.

EX. 633. Bizet—*L'Arlésienne*

The presence of the tendency tone brings out the inherent quality of the major tonic as dominant of the subdominant. Many examples are found of V₇ofIV with augmented fifth. Note the interval of the augmented sixth between the two upper voices as they are arranged in the following example.

EX. 634. Beethoven—*String Quartet, op. 18, no. 4*

C: V⁶₅ V²ofIV IV⁶ V⁶₅ofIV IV II I⁶₄ V⁷   I

In the following example of this chord, the upper voice, here first and second violins, divides into two parts, one of which proceeds upward by a diminished fourth to the tonic. The expansion of the number of voices to six adds to the expressive and colorful effect.

EX. 635. Strauss—*Till Eulenspiegel*

F: I   V⁷₅♯ofIV IV   I⁶₄

In dominant harmony the raised degree is the supertonic, suggesting the major mode by its implied resolution to the major third degree.

EX. 636

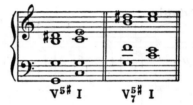

V⁵♯ I   V⁵♯₇ I

EX. 637. Brahms—*Pianoforte Concerto, op. 83*

The raised supertonic is a tendency tone added to those already present in the dominant seventh chord. Resolution of these tendency tones results in doubling the third of the tonic triad. The augmented sixth interval between two of the factors, as noted also in V₇ofIV, does not mean that these chords should be regarded as augmented sixth chords. The characteristic interval here is the augmented fifth, not the sixth.

EX. 638. Beethoven—*Symphony no. 9*

Added tendency reduces the number of practicable irregular resolutions. The student should try resolving this chord to all others and note examples of irregular resolution encountered in music. The following shows an effective resolution of the augmented triad V to the incomplete major ninth VofV.

EX. 639. Wagner—*Siegfried, Act III*

The subdominant chord with raised fifth differs rhythmically from the two chords described above in that it is nearly always an appoggiatura chord. The raised tonic is an appoggiatura to the second degree, and if seventh and ninth are present they act as appoggiature to the sixth and octave of a II chord in first inversion.

EX. 640

EX. 641. Liszt—*Pianoforte Sonata*

The augmented triad has a certain vagueness due to the fact that the inversions sound like the root position. It is composed of two major thirds which divide the octave into three equal parts, the upper interval—the diminished fourth—being the enharmonic equivalent of the major third. This symmetry suggests the origin of the whole-tone scale.

EX. 642

A succession of augmented triads loses the sense of definite tonality.

EX. 643. Liszt—*Dance of the Gnomes*

THE DIMINISHED FIFTH

Chromatic lowering of the fifth is found in dominant harmony. In the second inversion of the dominant seventh this produces a chord similar to the augmented six-four-three, but of dominant function.

EX. 644

EX. 645. Brahms—*Symphony no. 4*

This chord may resolve to a minor tonic as well.

EX. 646. Chopin—*Nocturne, op. 27, no. 1*

If this alteration (lowered second degree) is applied to the dominant minor ninth without root, the chord sounds like the augmented six-five-three but with dominant function. In this example it is heard over a tonic pedal:

EX. 647. Franck—*Quintet*

APPOGGIATURA CHORDS

It is customary to speak of a combination of appoggiature as an "appoggiatura chord." The name is retained here for want of a better general term, but it should be strongly emphasized that the chords commonly called appoggiatura chords most often form the weak part of a weak-to-strong progression, in which case the members could hardly be called appoggiature.

The method of forming these chords is that of preceding some or all of the factors of a given chord by tones a half step above or below, so that they resolve into the chord factors somewhat as leading-tones. The possibilities of forming new chords by this melodic process are very numerous and the individual combinations do not appear often enough to become part of the harmonic vocabulary, but a few characteristic examples can be given.

In the following example the first chord is an unusual form of IV$_7$, but its function is readily understood. Compare its effect with that of the raised submediant seventh as an introductory chord to the dominant.

EX. 648. Brahms—*Intermezzo, op. 116, no. 6*

When the subdominant triad appears with all its factors raised, to lead into the dominant, it becomes a chord whose root is distant from the tonic by an augmented fourth, the farthest possible.

EX. 649. Strauss—*Ein Heldenleben*

The following chord is like VI₇ except for the presence of the subdominant E.

EX. 650. Franck—*Prelude, Chorale, and Fugue*

It may so happen that the altered chord contains a factor which has been both raised and lowered.

EX. 651. Schubert—*Rosamunde*

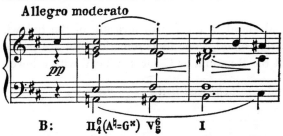

The following example shows a chord which might properly be called an appoggiatura chord because of the rhythm. It is questionable whether a weak-to-strong progression can be heard here, as the placing of the bar-line tends to suggest. The leading-tone in both chords creates a dominant feeling throughout.

EX. 652. Brahms—*Capriccio, op. 76, no. 8*

True appoggiatura chords are found in this example from Mozart, shown by asterisks. They are unquestionably harmonic in effect, but a root analysis seems less appropriate than a melodic description. Literally, both are augmented triads on the minor sixth degree, the third of the triad appearing simultaneously in both raised and un-altered form.

EX. 653. Mozart—*Symphony, K. 550*

The second chord in the fourth measure of the following may be called a passing chord, since its chromatic notes are passing tones. If we interpret the B-natural as C-flat it is VofV with a lowered fifth.

EX. 654. Brahms—*Schicksalslied*

The lowered tonic in the submediant triad, used by Franck as in the example below, imparts a dominant quality to the chord since it sounds like a leading-tone.

EX. 655. Franck—*Quintet*

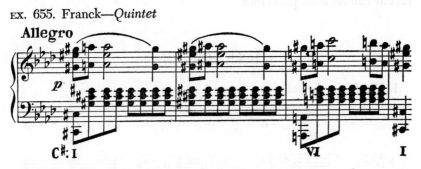

The raised subdominant seventh chord in the next example contains elements of VofV and of the raised VI.

EX. 656. Strauss—*Don Quixote*

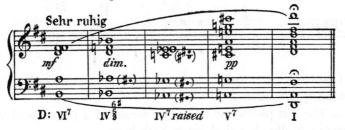

The examples given above by no means represent an exhaustive list of these altered chords, but they will serve to indicate the circumstances in which such chords appear. It is suggested that the student should record examples of similar chords discovered in music of the eighteenth and nineteenth centuries, taking special notice of those combinations found used several times.

MODULATION

As pivot chords, the chromatically altered forms have the disadvantage that since they are identified by their resolution it is necessary to establish carefully their position in the first key before giving them a second interpretation. On the other hand, the augmented triad is a versatile chord in modulation owing to its capacity for enharmonic change. The so-called appoggiatura chords can be effectively used whenever they are capable of interpretation as normal chords in the first key. For instance, the chord shown in Ex. 648 could be employed in a variety of modulations since it has the sound of a dominant seventh chord. Experimental studies in the modulatory possibilities of altered chords can be most profitable.

EXERCISES

1. Work out the following figured basses:

2. Construct a musical sentence of three phrases according to the following specifications:

a. The first phrase modulates by means of a pivot chord which is a chromatically altered chord in both keys.

b. The second phrase contains a modulating sequence whose pattern includes a dominant chord with lowered fifth. The phrase ends in a key not found in the first phrase.

c. The third phrase returns to the initial key by a pivot chord which is an augmented triad.

3. Harmonize the following unfigured basses, introducing chromatically altered chords:

4. Harmonize the following melodies, introducing chromatically altered chords:

Twenty-six | EXTENSION OF TONALITY

THE question of the extent to which chords may be related to a certain tonality, or whether or not a modulation has been brought about through the introduction of chromatic tones, will eventually be answered in analysis by the acceptance of all chords in any given key. This is not a necessary step, however, until the complexities of the twentieth century are reached in the study of harmony. But even in the period we have called the period of common practice, a broad concept of the domain of the tonal center is in keeping with the sense of music as heard. It has been seen that many chords containing notes foreign to the scale can be understood in their relationship to the prevailing tonal center.

The feeling of modulation, of complete change of tonal center, is received by the experienced ear with a certain inertia, together with a tendency to interpret the foreign harmony in terms of the key already established. When the key has not yet been established by a cadence or other clear tonal harmonies, as may be the case in the initial measures of a piece, these relationships will be discovered retroactively by analysis, if not by memory while listening, and they will be apparent on subsequent rehearing of the same music.

EXTENSION OF THE SECONDARY DOMINANT PRINCIPLE

Just as dominants of all degrees may be employed, other secondary tonal functions are made available through extension of the secondary dominant principle. In the following example, the G-minor triad is

related to the key of A as subdominant of the subdominant, and it may
be designated as IVofIV.

EX. 657. Brahms—*String Quartet, op. 51, no. 2*

A: I   III   IVofIV   IV   V

The minor triad on the fifth degree is quite lacking in dominant
feeling. When it stands in subdominant relationship to the supertonic
it may be called IVofII, as below.

EX. 658. Beethoven—*Symphony no. 9*

B♭: V   IVofII   II   IV   I$^6_4$

The diminished triad on D exists in B-flat as VofIV, but as used in
the example below the expression IIofII better describes its function
in the sequential harmony. To invoke a modulation to C minor on
account of this one triad would be to exaggerate its importance.

EX. 659. Krebs—*Minuet*

B♭: IIofII   VofII   II   V   I   V   I   V

False modulations to the key of the Neapolitan sixth suggest the
feasibility of the extension of the secondary principle in avoiding the

implication of a change of tonality when one is not felt to be significant. The example following contains the major triad built on the
augmented fourth above the tonic, a chord foreign to the tonality, but
used here as subdominant of F-flat major, the Neapolitan sixth. Enharmonic notation is frequently adopted, as it is here, to simplify the
reading of such chords as B-double-flat major.

EX. 660. Chopin—*Etude, op. 10, no. 6*

The tonal sense of the augmented sixth is so strong that in most
cases of its construction on roots other than II or IV its relationship
to the tonality is more accurately explained through extension of the
secondary dominant principle.

EX. 661. Haydn—*Symphony no. 101*

Similarly, a tonal unity can be shown in such passages as the following. It is plain that the composer does not intend the tonal center to
shift four times in these three bars. The augmented sixth chords with
their resolutions form a series of IV–V progressions standing for degrees of the key, namely the dominant E, subdominant D, and the
lowered seventh degree G, the latter being a modal step much used
by Grieg.

EX. 662. Grieg—*Solvejg's Song*

A: V   I(IVofV)   VofV IVofIV VofIV IVofVII VofVII IV   V
         (E min.)   (D min.)   (G min.)   (A min.)

The chord preceding a secondary dominant may be functionally closer to it than to the fundamental tonic. Mendelssohn's Wedding March begins with the formula II–V–I as of E minor, but, as everyone knows, the piece is in C major. The first chord is, then, properly designated as IIofIII rather than VofV in C.

EX. 663. Mendelssohn—*Midsummer Night's Dream: Wedding March*

C: II⁶₅ofIII V⁶ofIII   III   II⁶   I⁶₄   V⁷   I

The analysis of the next example goes a step further, in suggesting that VI of E, the second chord, take part in a grouping of four chords as of G-sharp minor, actually III of E.

EX. 664. Bach—*Chorale: Wie schön leuchtet der Morgenstern*

E: I IVofIII VofIII IVofIII III   IV⁶   I   V⁶₅ofV V⁷   I

In another Bach chorale three such groupings are shown, centering about III, VI, and IV of the fundamental key B-flat. The last chord in the second measure from the end, F minor, is obviously here IIofIV rather than V of B-flat, so that its dominant before it has been given the somewhat awkward but nonetheless accurate designation as VofIIofIV.

EX. 665. Bach—*Chorale: Ach Gott und Herr*

It has been recommended in this book that common groups of chords, or formulae, be perceived and remembered as units, like words, of musical meaning. Their recurrence in music often provides coherence, as in the following instance. The third, fourth, and fifth chords constitute a familiar half-cadence in A (see the sixth formula given in Chapter Twenty-three, page 288). Since the key is C, the symbol VI is substituted for A.

EX. 666. Wagner—*Die Walküre: Act III*

Four alternative analyses of the next example are presented for consideration of their relative merits.

EX. 667. Bach—*Well-tempered Clavier, I, Fugue no. 4*

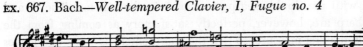

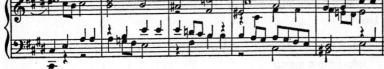

as modulating:

C♯: I {C♯: VI / E: IV} | V {E: I / B: IV} | V {B: I / F♯: IV} | V {F♯: I / C♯: IV} | V I |

literal roots in C♯:

C♯: I VI | VII III | IV VII | I IV | V I |

with secondary dominants:

C♯: I VI | VofIII III | ᐧ VofVII VII | VofIV IV | V I |

unitonal functions by extension of secondary dominant principle:

C♯: { I IV of →| IV of →| IV of →| IV (of) →| I
      VofIVofIVofIV | VofIVofIVofIV IVofIV | VofIV IV | V I
  { I IVofIVofIVofIV | IVofIVofIV | | }

Each analysis is correct from its own point of view, and it should be said that a preference for one should not mean a rejection of what the others may offer. The modulating sequence in *a* is clear at a glance, although one feels that the changes of tonal center happen too quickly, and that each key noted does not remain long enough to justify the analysis as a modulation. The pattern is not readily discernible in *b*, whereas *c* tells more about the grouping of the harmonies in the sequence. In *d* the organization of the passage is exactly set forth as in effect a step back from the tonic to a thrice removed subdominant, in order to return symmetrically by means of four IV–I progressions, with intervening dominants.

The freedom with which composers resort to enharmonic notation, to simplify reading for the performer, creates problems in analysis. The correct notation must first be determined from the voice-leading, and even this is not always possible. In the example below it is obvious that in the key of F-sharp the E-flat major triad, in measure three, should read D-sharp major, that is, VofII. The chord that precedes it and leads into it is the raised supertonic seventh of D-sharp, properly written with the double-sharps as shown in the scheme. The A and the F-sharp are, however, perfectly satisfactory as coming from the chords in the first measure, so that the chord enters as VofV and leaves as IIofVI.

EX. 668. Franck—*Sonata for Violin and Piano*

The next example contains a group of chords in flats, seeming on first sight to call for enharmonic reading, because of the signature of two sharps. The grouping has a dominant quality, as of the key of A-flat, which would be the lowered dominant of D. In measures four to six the harmony is based on the lowered supertonic (Neapoli-

EX. 669. Franck—*String Quartet*

tan), and forms a dominant ninth chord on this lowered II, dominant of the lowered V. The downward progression of this chord in measure six strengthens the conclusion that the notation is correct.

THE TWENTIETH CENTURY

The study of harmony in the twentieth century is not within the scope of this book. What has been summarized herein is the common harmonic practice of composers over a period of about two centuries. This practice forms the basis of the vast body of music to which we most often listen, and it represents the common ground of musical meaning by reference to which later developments should be studied and interpreted.

New ways of musical speech find more ready acceptance when they are understood as new aspects of musical meaning. The radically new has difficulty in finding acceptance because its connection with the common ground of musical meaning is not easily discerned. But experience shows that whatever lines of development from the past the most revolutionary musical speech may possess will become evident with time and acquaintance.

In the twentieth century new chords have been created by harmonic and contrapuntal means. Possibilities of unorthodox chromatic alterations have been explored, as well as methods of chord construction with intervals other than thirds. Chords have been formed by the synthesis of two or more existing chords. New harmonies have been found in the combination of nonharmonic tones with chords, especially in the principle of unresolved nonharmonic tones such as the appoggiatura.

The effort has been made to create music on a purely contrapuntal basis, without harmonic background, but since two or more tones sounding together make harmony this approach suffers from the presence of unwanted and undisciplined chordal meaning.

New and old scales and modes have been employed and some even invented, with interesting results, although they tend to be heard as variants of major-minor.

The period has been dominated by the idea that tonality, as generally understood, has outlived its usefulness as an organizing principle. Probably the most important musical event of the first half of the century was the emergence of the twelve-tone system, designed to replace the system of tonal functions by a serial technique involving tonal equality of all the twelve notes. It is a fact of experience that this music, as well as almost all music intended to be atonal, that is without key, comes sooner or later to be heard tonally. This is admittedly a regrettable violation of the composer's intentions, and it is due not only to an ingrained sense of tonality, but also to the circumstance that our daily musical contact is almost entirely with the strongly tonal music that is our heritage.

Newer organizing principles have been advanced, such as the creating of patterns of one musical element alone, for example rhythmic quantities only, dynamic levels only, or tone color only. Mathematical relationships between tones, inherent or imagined, have been exploited. Invention of the magnetic tape brought *musique concrète*, the manipulation of existing sounds by electronic means, and pure electronic music, in which the sound material itself is created by electronic means. Music has been produced by the electronic computer, and elements of chance have been the source material for composition.

Attractive and evocative new sounds have been discovered through these efforts. We are too near to them to be able to appraise their significance or determine their lines of development in the historical mainstream of musical meaning.

CONCLUSION

Each of the foregoing chapters has, of necessity, laid emphasis on the particular detail or aspect of harmonic procedure with which it was immediately concerned. The student's experience, then, will have been a series of changing impressions as to the comparative importance of each detail. Needless to say, the mastery of these details of common practice must be followed by an application of the set of principles as a whole. The most desirable program would be to complete the study of the material in the various chapters during the first year, devoting the second year to a study of the common practice of composers from a somewhat broader viewpoint, as well as to occasional review of details when that is needed.

It is recommended that the type of exercise drawn from actual compositions, described in Chapter Six, be extensively developed. The material should be judiciously selected, beginning with music that proceeds in normal fashion before introducing examples of unusual treatment. Exercises ought to be of considerable length, at least several phrases, so that experience will be afforded in problems of harmonic rhythm, modulation, phraseology, and the relation of the harmony to the form.

Some practice should be had in harmonic writing with three parts and with five parts. The student will use these media in his study of counterpoint, but there, the emphasis being on the lines, he will probably never use any but simple chords. No new principle is involved in arranging harmony for three or five voices. Comparison of examples of such writing with the basic four-part background will be helpful.

For exercises in harmonization, good material can be found in existing treatises, although as a rule the given parts are too short for the present purposes. Additional phrases can be constructed by the student to lengthen the exercises. Parts may be selected from standard works for harmonization and subsequent comparison with the composer's score. These parts may be soprano or bass, and for variety even an inner voice may be taken so that both soprano and bass are to be constructed.

When a fair degree of facility in manipulating the harmonic material is achieved, some writing may be done in instrumental style, for the piano or for combinations of instruments. It is well to insist, however, that the prime object is the study of harmonic practice rather than of idiomatic instrumental writing.

Finally, on the basis of a secure knowledge of the common practice of composers in the eighteenth and nineteenth centuries, one turns to the application of this norm as a means for further harmonic study in two main directions. The first of these directions is toward the study of the individual practices of the individual composers during the period, represented by their departures from, or conformity with, the norm of common practice. The second is the investigation, in much the same way, of harmonic procedure in the twentieth century. Here the evolutionary aspect should be stressed, effort being made to uncover the lines of development from the norm of common practice to the new means employed.

The writer is aware that what has been outlined briefly in a few sentences amounts to virtually an endless assignment. It is not to be denied that the acquisition of a consummate knowledge of the practice of composers is a lifetime's work. *Ars longa, vita brevis,* but consolation may be derived from the thought that intellectual and artistic rewards are to be had at all stages along the way.

SUPPLEMENTARY EXERCISES

CHAPTER ONE

1. Name the following intervals:

2. For each of the following intervals, determine the scale which contains both tones. More than one scale is to be found for each interval.

3. For each of the following four-note fragments, determine the scale which contains all four notes:

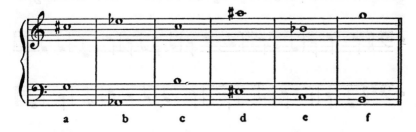

CHAPTER TWO

Keeping in each case the note G-sharp as top note of the triad, write in four parts the following chord forms:

  a. a major triad in first inversion, with its fifth in the soprano
  b. a dissonant triad with its third in the soprano
  c. a triad in second inversion, in the key of E
  d. a triad whose root is the mediant of a minor scale
  e. a triad in open position, with its root in the soprano
  f. a minor triad in close position
  g. an augmented triad with its third doubled
  h. a consonant triad in the key of B minor
  i. a diminished triad in major mode
  j. a triad in first inversion, with subdominant in the bass

CHAPTER THREE

Add soprano, alto, and tenor parts to the following basses, making four-part harmony. Use only triads in root position, and work out two versions for each given bass.

CHAPTER FOUR

1. In which tonalities is E-flat a modal degree? a tonal degree? Answer the same questions for the notes F-sharp, B, G-sharp, and D-flat.

2. Rewrite the following progressions, changing those that are major to minor, and those that are minor to major.

CHAPTER FIVE

1. Write out the four-part harmony indicated by the following figured basses.

2. Harmonize the following unfigured bass, introducing chords of the sixth where appropriate.

3. Harmonize the following melodies, using triads in root position and in first inversion.

CHAPTER SIX

Harmonize the following basses in four parts, using triads in root position. In these exercises pay particular attention to the differentiation of harmonic and melodic rhythms.

CHAPTER SEVEN

1. Harmonize the following soprano melodies, using triads in root position and first inversion.

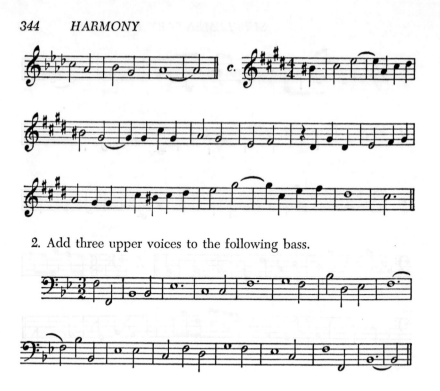

2. Add three upper voices to the following bass.

CHAPTER EIGHT

1. Work out the following figured basses in four parts.

A straight line placed after a figure means that the note represented by the figure is maintained in the harmony to the end of the line, regardless of the change of bass. For example, in the first measure of the first given bass the tonic triad in first inversion is indicated for two beats of the measure. In the second measure the figures call for the notes A and E, so the harmony is dominant and the D is seen to be a suspension. Other nonharmonic tones may be introduced in addition to those indicated by the figures. Roman numerals identifying the root should be placed under each chord in all exercises. Attention is called to the modulation to the dominant key in the second given bass.

2. Harmonize the following soprano and bass parts, after careful analysis to determine which tones are to be interpreted as non-harmonic.

CHAPTER NINE

1. Work out the following figured basses in four parts.

2. Harmonize the following soprano and bass parts. At least five six-four chords are to be introduced into each exercise.

CHAPTER TEN

1. Work out the following figured basses in four parts.

2. Harmonize the following bass and soprano parts, after analyzing them to decide upon the types of cadences they contain.

CHAPTER ELEVEN

Harmonize the following basses in four parts.

CHAPTER TWELVE

Harmonize the following basses and soprano melodies, using only triads in root position. The location of the pivot chord for each modulation is shown by *.

CHAPTER THIRTEEN

1. Work out the following figured basses in four parts.

2. Harmonize the following bass and soprano parts, introducing dominant seventh chords where appropriate. Use at least eight dominant seventh chords in each exercise.

CHAPTER FOURTEEN

1. Work out the following figured basses.

2. Harmonize the following bass and soprano parts, employing secondary dominant chords where appropriate.

CHAPTER FIFTEEN

1. Work out the following figured basses.

2. Harmonize the following bass and soprano parts, introducing irregular resolutions of dominant seventh chords and of secondary dominants.

CHAPTER SIXTEEN

1. Work out the following figured bass.

2. Harmonize the following bass and soprano parts, introducing diminished seventh chords at *.

3. Harmonize the following bass and soprano parts, employing diminished seventh chords where appropriate.

CHAPTER SEVENTEEN

1. Work out the following figured bass.

2. Harmonize the following bass and soprano parts. At * use incomplete major ninth chords.

CHAPTER EIGHTEEN

1. Work out the following figured bass.

2. Harmonize the following bass and soprano parts. At * use complete dominant ninth chords.

CHAPTER NINETEEN

1. Work out the following figured basses.

2. Harmonize the following basses, the first modulating, the second nonmodulating.

3. Harmonize the following soprano melodies containing modulating sequences.

CHAPTER TWENTY

1. Work out the following figured basses.

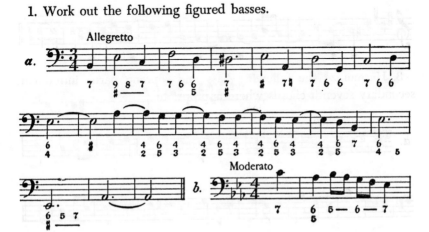

2. Harmonize the following bass and soprano parts. At * use secondary seventh chords.

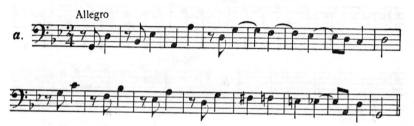

3. Harmonize the following bass and soprano parts, introducing secondary seventh chords where appropriate.

CHAPTER TWENTY-ONE

1. Work out the following figured bass.

2. Harmonize the following bass and soprano parts. At * introduce a ninth, eleventh, or thirteenth chord effect.

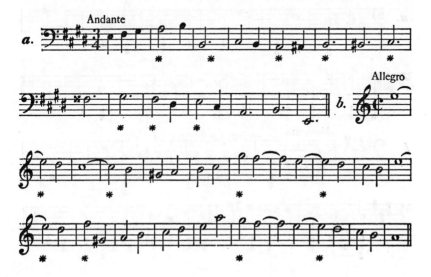

3. Harmonize the following bass and soprano parts, using ninth, eleventh, and thirteenth chord effects where appropriate.

CHAPTER TWENTY-TWO

1. Work out the following figured basses.

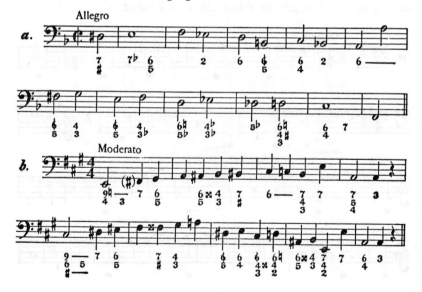

2. Harmonize the following bass and soprano parts. At * use chords of the raised supertonic or submediant.

CHAPTER TWENTY-THREE

1. Work out the following figured basses.

2. Harmonize the following bass and soprano parts. At * use Neapolitan sixth chords.

CHAPTER TWENTY-FOUR

1. Work out the following figured basses.

2. Harmonize the following bass and soprano parts. At * use chords of the augmented sixth.

CHAPTER TWENTY-FIVE

1. Work out the following figured basses.

2. Harmonize the following bass and soprano parts. Introduce chromatically altered chords wherever practicable and possible of explanation by reference to the principles of common practice harmony.

Index